The German Americans

Consulting Editors

THE IMMIGRANT EXPERIENCE

The German Americans

Anne Galicich

Sandra Stotsky, General Editor
Harvard University Graduate School of Education

CHELSEA HOUSE PUBLISHERS

New York • Philadelphia

CHELSEA HOUSE PUBLISHERS

Editorial Director: Richard Rennert
Executive Managing Editor: Karyn Gullen Browne
Copy Chief: Robin James
Picture Editor: Adrian G. Allen
Creative Director: Robert Mitchell
Art Director: Joan Ferrigno
Production Manager: Sallye Scott

THE IMMIGRANT EXPERIENCE

Editors: Mary Barr Sisson and Reed Ueda

Staff for THE GERMAN AMERICANS

Assistant Editor: Annie McDonnell
Copy Editor: Apple Kover
Assistant Designer: Stephen Schildbach
Cover Illustrator: Jane Sterrett

3 5 7 9 8 6 4 2

Library of Congress Cataloging-in-Publication Data

Galicich, Anne.
The German Americans / Anne Galicich ; Sandra Stotsky, general editor.
p. cm.—(The immigrant experience)
Includes bibliographical references and index.
Summary: Discusses the history, culture, and religion of the Germans, factors encouraging their emigration, and their acceptance as the United States' largest ethnic group.
ISBN 0-7910-3362-7.
0-7910-3384-8 (pbk.)
1. German Americans—Juvenile literature. [1. German Americans.] I. Stotsky, Sandra. II. Title. III. Series.
E184.G3G15 1995 95-31685
973'.0431—dc20 CIP
AC

Contents

THE IMMIGRANT EXPERIENCE

A LAND OF IMMIGRANTS
THE AFRICAN AMERICANS
THE AMERICAN INDIANS
THE AMISH
THE ARAB AMERICANS
THE CHINESE AMERICANS
THE CUBAN AMERICANS
THE GERMAN AMERICANS
THE GREEK AMERICANS
THE HAITIAN AMERICANS
ILLEGAL ALIENS
THE IRISH AMERICANS
THE ITALIAN AMERICANS
THE JAPANESE AMERICANS
THE JEWISH AMERICANS
THE KOREAN AMERICANS
THE LEBANESE CHRISTIANS
THE MEXICAN AMERICANS
THE POLISH AMERICANS
THE PUERTO RICANS
THE RUSSIAN AMERICANS
Other titles in preparation

CHELSEA HOUSE PUBLISHERS

A NATION OF NATIONS

DANIEL PATRICK MOYNIHAN

The Constitution of the United States begins: "We the People of the United States. . ." Yet, as we know, the United States was not then and is not now made up of a single group of people. It is made up of many peoples. Immigrants and bondsmen from Europe, Asia, Africa, and Central and South America came here or were brought here, and still they come. They forged one nation and made it their own. More than 100 years ago, Walt Whitman expressed this great central fact of America: "Here is not merely a nation, but a teeming Nation of nations."

Although the ingenuity and acts of courage of these immigrants, our ancestors, shaped the North American way of life, we sometimes take their contributions for granted. This fine series, *The Peoples of North America*, examines the experiences and contributions of different immigrant groups and how these contributions determined the future of the United States and Canada.

Immigrants did not abandon their ethnic traditions when they reached the shores of North America. Each ethnic group had its own customs and traditions, and each brought different experiences, accomplishments, skills, values, styles of dress, and tastes in food that lingered long after its arrival. Yet this profusion of differences created a singularity, or bond, among the immigrants.

The United States and Canada are unusual in this respect. Whereas religious and ethnic differences have sparked intolerance throughout the rest of the world—from the 17th-century religious wars to the 19th-century nationalist movements in Europe to the near extermination of the Jewish people under Nazi Germany—North Americans have struggled to learn how to respect each other's differences and live in harmony.

Our two countries are hardly the only two in which different groups must learn to live together. There is no nation of significant size anywhere in the world which would not be classified as multiethnic. But only in North America are there so *many* different groups, most of them living cheek by jowl with one another.

This is not easy. Look around the world. And it has not always been easy for us. Witness the exclusion of Chinese immigrants, and for practical purposes Japanese also, in the late 19th century. But by the late 20th century, Chinese and Japanese Americans were the most successful of all the groups recorded by the census. We have had prejudice aplenty, but it has been resisted and recurrently overcome.

The remarkable ability of Americans to live together as one people was seriously threatened by the issue of slavery. Thousands of settlers from the British Isles had arrived in the colonies as indentured servants, agreeing to work for a specified number of years on farms or as apprentices in return for passage to America and room and board. When the first Africans arrived in the then-British colonies during the 17th century, some colonists thought that they too should be treated as indentured servants. Eventually, the question of whether the Africans should be treated as indentured, like the English, or as slaves who could be owned for life was considered in a Maryland court. The court's calamitous decree held that blacks were slaves bound to a lifelong servitude, and so also were their children. America went through a time of moral examination and civil war before it finally freed African slaves and their descendants. The principle that all people are created equal had faced its greatest challenge and survived.

Yet the court ruling that set blacks apart from other races fanned flames of discrimination that burned long after slavery was abolished—and that still flicker today. Indeed, it was about the time of the American Civil War that European theories of evolution were turned to the service of ranking different peoples by their presumed distance from our apelike ancestors.

When the Irish flooded American cities to escape the famine in Ireland, the cartoonists caricatured the typical "Paddy" (a common term for Irish immigrants) as an apelike creature with jutting jaw and sloping forehead.

By the 20th century, racism and ethnic prejudice had given rise to virulent theories of a Northern European master race. When Adolf Hitler came to power in Germany in 1933, he popularized the notion of an Aryan race. Only a man of the deepest ignorance and evil could have done this. *Aryan* is a Sanskrit word, which is to say the ancient script of what we now think of as India. It means "noble" and was adopted by linguists—notably by a fine German scholar, Max Müller—to denote the Indo-European family of languages. Müller was horrified that anyone could think of it in terms of race, especially a race of blond-haired, blue-eyed Teutons. But the Nazis embraced the notion of a master race. Anyone with darker and heavier features was considered inferior. Buttressed by these theories, the German Nazi state from 1933 to 1945 set out to destroy European Jews, along with Poles, Gypsies, Russians, and other groups considered inferior. It nearly succeeded. Millions of these people were murdered.

The tragedies brought on by ethnic and racial intolerance throughout the world demonstrate the importance of North America's efforts to create a society free of prejudice and inequality.

A relatively recent example of the New World's desire to resolve ethnic friction nonviolently is the solution that the Canadians found to a conflict between two ethnic groups. A long-standing dispute as to whether Canadian culture was properly English or French resurfaced in the mid-1960s, dividing the peoples of the French-speaking Province of Quebec from those of the English-speaking provinces. Relations grew tense, then bitter, then violent. The Royal Commission on Bilingualism and Biculturalism was established to study the growing crisis and to propose measures to ease the tensions. As a result of the commission's recommendations, all official documents and statements from the national government's capital at Ottawa are now issued in both French and English, and bilingual education is encouraged.

The year 1980 marked a coming of age for the United States's ethnic heritage. For the first time, the U.S. Bureau of the Census asked people about their ethnic background. Americans chose from more than 100 groups, including French Basque, Spanish Basque, French Canadian, African-American, Peruvian, Armenian, Chinese, and Japanese. The ethnic group with the largest response was English (49.6 million). More than 100 million Americans claimed ancestors from the British Isles, which includes England, Ireland, Wales, and Scotland. There were almost as many Germans (49.2 million) as English. The Irish-American population (40.2 million) was third, but the next-largest ethnic group, the African-Americans, was a distant fourth (21 million). There was a sizable group of French ancestry (13 million) as well as of Italian (12 million). Poles, Dutch, Swedes, Norwegians, and Russians followed. These groups, and other smaller ones, represent the wondrous profusion of ethnic influences in North America.

Canada too has learned more about the diversity of its population. Studies conducted during the French/English conflict showed that Canadians were descended from Ukrainians, Germans, Italians, Chinese, Japanese, native Indians, and Inuit, among others. Canada found it had no ethnic majority, although nearly half of its immigrant population had come from the British Isles. Canada, like the United States, is a land of immigrants for whom mutual tolerance is a matter of reason as well as principle. But note how difficult this can be in practice, even for persons of manifest goodwill.

The people of North America are the descendants of one of the greatest migrations in history. And that migration is not over.

Koreans, Vietnamese, Nicaraguans, Cubans, and many others are heading for the shores of North America in large numbers. This mix of cultures shapes every aspect of our lives. To understand ourselves, we must know something about our diverse ethnic ancestry. Nothing so defines the North American nations as the motto on the Great Seal of the United States: *E Pluribus Unum*—Out of Many, One.

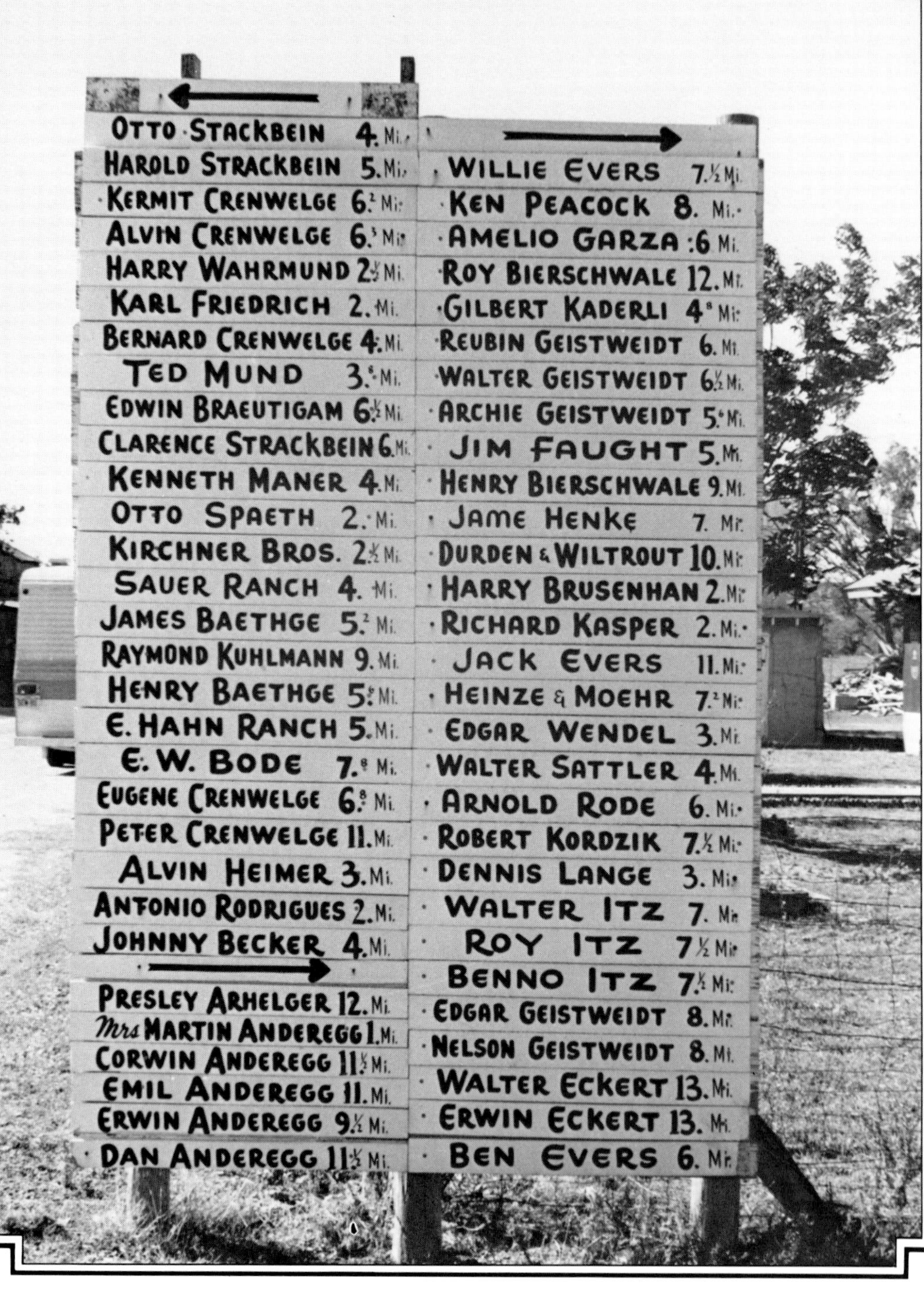
OTTO STACKBEIN 4. Mi.
HAROLD STRACKBEIN 5. Mi.
KERMIT CRENWELGE 6.2 Mi.
ALVIN CRENWELGE 6.3 Mi.
HARRY WAHRMUND 2½ Mi.
KARL FRIEDRICH 2. Mi.
BERNARD CRENWELGE 4. Mi.
TED MUND 3.6 Mi.
EDWIN BRAEUTIGAM 6½ Mi.
CLARENCE STRACKBEIN 6. Mi.
KENNETH MANER 4. Mi.
OTTO SPAETH 2. Mi.
KIRCHNER BROS. 2½ Mi.
SAUER RANCH 4. Mi.
JAMES BAETHGE 5.2 Mi.
RAYMOND KUHLMANN 9. Mi.
HENRY BAETHGE 5.8 Mi.
E. HAHN RANCH 5. Mi.
E. W. BODE 7.8 Mi.
EUGENE CRENWELGE 6.8 Mi.
PETER CRENWELGE 11. Mi.
ALVIN HEIMER 3. Mi.
ANTONIO RODRIGUES 2. Mi.
JOHNNY BECKER 4. Mi.
PRESLEY ARHELGER 12. Mi.
Mrs MARTIN ANDEREGG 1. Mi.
CORWIN ANDEREGG 11½ Mi.
EMIL ANDEREGG 11. Mi.
ERWIN ANDEREGG 9½ Mi.
DAN ANDEREGG 11½ Mi.
WILLIE EVERS 7½ Mi.
KEN PEACOCK 8. Mi.
AMELIO GARZA 6 Mi.
ROY BIERSCHWALE 12. Mi.
GILBERT KADERLI 4.8 Mi.
REUBIN GEISTWEIDT 6. Mi.
WALTER GEISTWEIDT 6½ Mi.
ARCHIE GEISTWEIDT 5.6 Mi.
JIM FAUGHT 5. Mi.
HENRY BIERSCHWALE 9. Mi.
JAME HENKE 7. Mi.
DURDEN & WILTROUT 10. Mi.
HARRY BRUSENHAN 2. Mi.
RICHARD KASPER 2. Mi.
JACK EVERS 11. Mi.
HEINZE & MOEHR 7.2 Mi.
EDGAR WENDEL 3. Mi.
WALTER SATTLER 4. Mi.
ARNOLD RODE 6. Mi.
ROBERT KORDZIK 7½ Mi.
DENNIS LANGE 3. Mi.
WALTER ITZ 7. Mi.
ROY ITZ 7½ Mi.
BENNO ITZ 7½ Mi.
EDGAR GEISTWEIDT 8. Mi.
NELSON GEISTWEIDT 8. Mi.
WALTER ECKERT 13. Mi.
ERWIN ECKERT 13. Mi.
BEN EVERS 6. Mi.

A signpost in rural Texas displays a wealth of German names. Eighteen percent of the American populace now claims full or partial German descent.

STRENGTH IN NUMBERS

Almost any list of Americans—the roster of a baseball team, a class attendance sheet, a telephone book—includes a large number of German names. Some are not obviously German (Houser, Newman, or Berger), and often even the individual who bears the name is not certain of its origin. Americans of most ethnic backgrounds have intermarried to such an extent that about two-thirds now claim multiple ancestry, and German Americans are no exception.

In 1986, according to the U.S. Census Bureau, for the first time in more than 300 years the leading ancestral background of America's residents was no longer British, but German. Roughly 44 million Americans, or 18 percent of the populace, claimed sole or partial German heritage, a few hundred thousand more than claimed British descent.

Because the German-American population is so large, it is hard to generalize about it. Americans of German descent spring up in virtually every occupation, live in every state, and hold a spectrum of political and religious beliefs. In short, they typify America. Indeed, the vast majority are Americans of long standing; only 4 percent of today's 44 million German Americans were born in Germany.

The term *German American* encompasses a number of peoples. Before 1871, Germany was not a nation, but a collection of dozens of small states, duchies, kingdoms, and principalities, each with its own ruler, customs, and regional dialect. Over seven centuries speckled with migrations, wars, and religious conflict, these lands covered much of north-central Europe, from the North Sea to the Nieman River near Kaunas, Lithuania. So speakers of German came from what are now parts of Denmark, the Netherlands, Belgium, Luxembourg, France, Switzerland, Austria, Hungary, Czechoslovakia, Poland, and the Soviet Union. Immigration officials in the New World sometimes listed people as Germans although Germany was not their land of origin. If the annals of history have sometimes lumped diverse people under one umbrella term—*German*—it is a simplification we must now acknowledge, if not embrace.

Present from the Inception

Beginning in 1683, Germans formed the first substantial group of non-English-speaking immigrants to settle in America. By the outbreak of the revolutionary war in 1776, their numbers had reached 225,000. More so than most other ethnic groups, who arrived in the 19th and 20th centuries, German immigrants have had more time to adapt, intermarry, and to disperse throughout the nation.

The revolutionary war and subsequent conflicts in both America and Europe slowed immigration, but Germans continued to sail to these shores. Beginning in the late 1830s, they came to America in record numbers, surpassed only by the Irish. They thereby retained their status as the largest non-English-speaking group. In 1882 alone, a quarter of a million Germans arrived in the United States.

The Germans who arrived during this later period (1816–90) differed in several ways from those who had arrived earlier. Whereas most German immigrants of the 18th century came from the Palatine or Württem-

Between 1866 and 1871, Germany was unified politically from a score of smaller states and duchies. Natives of each district were loyal to their home region, and even today German Americans may name Bavaria or Saxony, rather than Germany, as their land of origin. After World War II, the country was partitioned into communist-run East Germany and democratically governed West Germany, a division that lasted until October 1990, when the country was reunited as the Federal Republic of Germany under a democratic form of government.

Note: Political states within Germany do not all correspond with historical regions.

A turn-of-the-century immigrant in traditional German dress at Ellis Island in New York harbor. Today, about 44 million Americans can claim partial or full German ancestry, making them the country's largest ethnic group.

berg, states along the Rhine River in the southern and western regions of the German lands, those in the second wave of immigration came mainly from the north and east—Prussia, Bavaria, and Saxony.

Those who came before 1871, the year Germany was unified, tended to be loyal to their particular state or locality, rather than to Germany as a whole. Thus, Germans were not inclined to bond as one identifiable group in the United States. Even today, a recent German immigrant may refer to him- or herself as a Saxon, Bavarian, or Berliner.

German immigrants came not only from all parts of Germany but also from all walks of life and for many different reasons. In the 18th century, religious persecution prompted many emigrants to cross the Atlantic, often in groups—families, parishes, and sometimes entire communities traveled together. In the 19th century, political oppression at home encouraged many idealistic and utopian plans for a free colony of Germans in the United States. These new immigrants were often better educated and more politically minded than their predecessors.

Still, the overwhelming majority of immigrants came in search of better economic opportunities. In the years before the Civil War, German newcomers tended to be independent craftsmen or farmers and their families, who could afford the cost of passage and could meet the demands of the developing and still largely agricultural countries of the United States and Canada. After the Civil War, the rapid growth of industry in America and the advent of the more convenient and affordable steamship enticed German day laborers who had no families and no special skills.

The 20th century created yet another sort of immigrant, the wartime refugee, especially just before and during World War II. The total number of refugees was comparatively small, but they made an impact in the sciences, business, and the arts. Many were Jews, who were joined by Catholics, Protestants, and others

The German infant school in St. Peter, Minnesota, 1867. In addition to starting the first kindergartens in the New World, Germans have contributed substantially to American business, music, science, agriculture, art, and sports.

who professed no religion, in fleeing Hitler's regime of 1933–45.

Events in America served to divide further a population that had already been broken up along religious, class, and territorial lines. Because they arrived during different periods and at a variety of ports, German immigrants settled all over the United States. Many gravitated to cities, where they blended into the general population more quickly than they would have in the countryside. Though German Americans are now dispersed across the continent, their history and culture figure most evidently in a handful of strongholds: St. Louis, Cincinnati, Milwaukee, Philadelphia, and parts of the Middle Atlantic states and the upper Midwest. (The fabled Pennsylvania Dutch are not Dutch but Germans, whose name for themselves, *Deutsche*, was misunderstood by their Yankee neighbors.) In those locales they have long been the dominant group, though fierce anti-German sentiment aroused by World War I effectively discouraged German cohesiveness in all but the sturdiest of their communities.

The sheer number of German immigrants, their 300 years of immigration, their diversity in class, religion, and occupation, and their experiences in the United States have all played a role in their rapid assimilation and subsequent lack of visibility. Yet these same factors have also allowed them to influence American culture in a multitude of ways.

In 1683 a group of 34 immigrants from the city of Krefeld founded Germantown, now part of Philadelphia, Pennsylvania; their leader called them "the forerunners of all German colonists."

IN THE COLONIES

When Francis Daniel Pastorius, in his words, "laid out and planned a new town . . . in a very fine and fertile district" outside Philadelphia in 1683, he allotted each house three acres of land and reserved six for himself as the community leader. The new town was Germantown, bordered by the Wissahickon and the Wingohocking creeks, and its layout resembled the medieval villages of southwest Germany. Through its center ran a single 60-foot-wide road, along which every resident built a home; behind each house stretched the owner's garden and fields.

The Germantown residents came at the invitation of William Penn, Quaker governor of Pennsylvania (Penn's woods). The Quakers, also known as the Society of Friends, had got their start in England in the late 1640s; they are plain of dress and peaceable in their beliefs and were prominent in the early settling of Pennsylvania. Penn had received the province in 1681 as a gift from King Charles II of England and immediately set about finding settlers for it. He wrote a pamphlet giving the terms of this "Holy Experiment," and Benjamin Furly, a Dutch merchant and fellow Quaker, translated the tract into German so that it could be distributed throughout the Rhineland. The prospect of cheap land—and, more important, religious tolerance—caught the imagination of 13 families in Krefeld, a German town near the Dutch border. In Frankfurt-am-Main, it stirred Pastorius to action.

When he read of Penn's offer, in November 1682, Pastorius had been in Frankfurt only a short time. His father was mayor of the town of Windsheim, where Pastorius returned after his university studies to establish a law practice. But law soon bored him. It seemed, he wrote, to be "a game at another's expense." Frankfurt was not enough of a change, so he and a friend embarked on a tour of Europe.

The "European idleness" that he encountered on this trip greatly troubled Pastorius. He wrote that he had seen

> many thousand young Germans, mostly of the nobility, who are accustomed to follow the vanities of dress, speech, foreign manners and ceremonies, and incur incredible expense in learning to mount, to ride, to dance, to fence . . . while not a single thought is given to the love of God and learning to follow Christ.

This extravagance was supported by taxes paid by common citizens.

Disillusioned, Pastorius returned to Frankfurt, where a group of friends suggested that he accept Penn's offer. He received the plan enthusiastically, soon acting as a land agent to buy 15,000 acres from Penn at the bargain price of about 10 cents per acre. Pastorius

In the 17th and 18th centuries, German princes routinely rode and hunted; common people, however, were forbidden to kill most game. The class system's injustice, religious intolerance, and the ravages of war prompted Francis Pastorius and thousands of Germans like him to seek a fresh start in the New World.

The Thirty Years' War (1618–48), fought between Protestant and Catholic forces across Europe, destroyed many German towns and farms. Such chaos as the massacre in the city of Magdeburg in 1631, shown here, epitomized the plight of the citizenry.

wrote that he was anxious to travel to America, to establish a colony in the wilderness "far from the wickedness, strifes, and persecutions which distressed the godly in Europe."

When Pastorius wrote these words, distress was endemic in Europe. In times of peace, southwest Germany, fed by the Rhine, Neckar, and Main rivers, was fertile farmland. But the Thirty Years' War (1618–48), the culmination of a century of political and religious disputes that came to involve most of the European powers, had devastated the region. German peasants paid for their princes' palaces but lived their own lives on a battleground.

In 1517 German theologian Martin Luther had fired the first salvo against the religious and political supremacy of the Catholic church by listing church abuses he thought needed reform. The Lutheran church quickly gained members, in an era that came to be called the Protestant Reformation. But the Peace of Augsburg in 1555 gave official sanction only to Catholicism and Lutheranism (then the largest branch of Protestantism), not yet recognizing other growing Protestant creeds such as the Calvinist (Reformed) movement or the Anabaptists.

Now, during the Thirty Years' War, Catholic princes warred with Protestant princes. In the county of Henneberg alone, 75 percent of the inhabitants were slaughtered, and 66 percent of the houses were burned to the ground. Foreign armies and bands of thieves and beggars roamed from village to village stealing and conscripting men into their armies. There were even reports of cannibalism.

The Founding of Germantown

In the wake of such chaos, Germans must have imagined the New World as paradise, as this emigrant's letter amply illustrates:

> Those who do not know hunger and need cannot comprehend why thousands of people undertake the voyage. The complaints about the government are legion! Work is no longer of any help in making a living—in a situation like this people become truly desperate. . . . We are told that those who want to go to Prussia will get travel money and land as in America, but what is a free man compared to a slave or serf?

By the time the Krefelders left in 1683, there existed in southwest Germany not only a long tradition of disruption and difficulty but also a tradition of *Auswanderung*, or "wandering out." Many people moved from state to state within Germany; others crossed the border to Switzerland; others made it to Holland, from where many of them took ship for America. In fact, the first settlers to join Pastorius in Pennsylvania were probably relocated Dutch. Twelve were Quakers, one of whom—Jacob Telner—had visited Pennsylvania and returned to his hometown to persuade others to join him. Aided by Benjamin Furly, who arranged their passage on the *Concord*, the Krefelders embarked on a route that thousands would eventually follow: down the Rhine to Rotterdam, across the English Channel to London, and then across the Atlantic.

The Krefelders were lucky. According to an English Quaker merchant who accompanied them on their journey, "The blessing of the Lord did attend us so that we had a very comfortable passage, and had our health all the way." The *Concord* docked in Philadelphia on October 6, 1683, three months after Pastorius had arrived. They soon converged on the cave that was Pastorius's temporary home and drew lots for their three-acre plots of land.

Pastorius called these 34 original settlers the "forerunners of all German colonists." Historians have since tended to agree: Though scattered German immigrants had reached the 13 colonies earlier, the founding of Germantown, Pennsylvania, is widely recognized as the birth of the history of Germans in America. After 1683, Germantown grew rapidly: from 13 families at its start to 64 families "in a very prosperous condition" in 1700, to 556 families, or 3,000 people, in 1790, after the American Revolution. The population in and around Germantown included Germans from all states (though the principalities most well represented were Palatine and Württemberg) and other German-speaking peoples (Swiss, Austrians, and some relocated Dutch).

The meandering back roads and steeply pitched roofs common in the earliest days of Germantown bore a marked resemblance to those of medieval towns in southwestern Germany, the first settlers' home region.

In 1698, Pastorius wrote that "the inhabitants of this city are for the most part tradespeople, such as cloth, fustian [coarse flaxen cloth], and linen weavers, tailors, shoemakers, locksmiths, carpenters." By 1773 a list of 120 men included 28 assorted occupations, including dyers, millers, blacksmiths, brass founders, tanners, saddlers, and other leather crafters. By 1800 the Germantown vicinity boasted eight grist mills (for processing wheat), a sawmill, a corn mill, and a chocolate maker. Farmers rode to market in locally made Conestoga wagons. Named after a creek in the area, these linen-covered wagons were drawn by a team of horses and would later play a major role in thousands of Americans' westward trek.

Germantown residents tended to be artisans (known then as mechanics) rather than merchants, so their places of business were usually workshops, not stores. In Germany, where trades were monitored by associations called guilds, craftsmen faced a variety of restrictions; in America, there were none. Gottfried Mittelberger marveled in 1750 that "if any could or would carry on ten trades, no one would have a right to prevent him." And some did. Christopher Saur was a stonemason, farmer, wheelwright, and clockmaker before settling down at a printing press to publish a successful newspaper, religious pamphlets, and farmers' almanac in German.

Though Germantown itself was never a predominantly agricultural community (it was absorbed by Philadelphia in 1847), the surrounding area (and the other colonies, as well) was mostly peopled by farmers, known then as "husbandmen" or "vine dressers." Benjamin Rush, a physician who wrote *An Account of the Manners of the German Inhabitants of Pennsylvania* in 1798, recorded how the German farmers developed an excellent reputation. "The German farm," he wrote, "was easily distinguished from those of others, by good fences, the extent of the orchard, the fertility of soil, productiveness of the fields, the luxuriance of the mead-

The Conestoga wagon, which got its name from a creek near the Germantown shop of its manufacture, helped farmers get their crops to market. Farming dominated the area around Germantown; townsmen were mainly artisans in such trades as carpentry, weaving, and masonry.

ows." German farmers are credited today with introducing diversified farming (the practice of planting more than one type of crop), crop rotation, and the use of barnyard manure, red clover, and gypsum (sulphate of lime) as fertilizers. German farmers also cleared their land thoroughly, rather than following the English practice of "girdling," or cutting into the trees so they would die in the fields. Such forethought, including the choice of prime limestone areas (for easy drainage) on which to settle, earned these farmers their reputation, and the area in which they lived became known as "the heart of American grain production."

"A Quiet, Godly, and Honest Life"

A great part of the attraction of Pennsylvania lay in William Penn's original promise of religious tolerance. In his preamble to the Germantown laws, Pastorius made reference to the importance of this freedom in the establishment of the community. Foremost among Pastorius's own reasons for emigrating was the "desire in [his] soul to lead a quiet, godly, and honest life in a howling wilderness."

Others after him came with the same intent. From 1683 to about 1727, most of the arrivals were Quakers. Other religious sects proved to be ephemeral, lasting only as long as their charismatic leaders lived. A few congregations were better established and had persisted for decades or even centuries in Europe's increasingly hostile climate.

The sect members were acutely aware of their past persecution. The Mennonites, descendants of Anabaptists (so named because of their belief in adult baptism), arrived carrying the *Martyrs' Mirror*, a holy book that relates the story of their ancestors' sufferings. Included in this history is the Catholic church edict of 1520 that all Anabaptists be put to death without a trial; during the Peasant Wars of 1524–25, more than 50,000 Anabaptists were killed. Survivors scattered, later to be united through the efforts of Menno Simons, a Roman Catholic priest who left the church in 1536 (and for whom the Mennonites are named). The Amish, who broke off from the Mennonites, have a book of 140 hymns called the *Ausbund*, which also celebrates the sufferings of the Anabaptist martyrs. The belief in nonviolence, shared by the Mennonites, the Amish, and the Quakers, sprang in part from their memory of violence suffered at the hands of others.

A baptism of Indians by Moravians, 1757. Pennsylvania was founded on the principle of religious tolerance, a "Godly and honest" place for Quakers, Lutherans, Reformed, Amish, Jews, Mennonites, and other denominations.

In the 18th century, the arduous, sometimes fatal, voyage from Germany to the New World usually began in Rotterdam, the Netherlands, and stopped in London. This ship, the London Merchant, *sailed in 1734 with 257 German Protestants bound for the colony of Georgia.*

In general, the sects stressed a direct relationship to God, rather than one mediated by the clergy. They believed that worship should be entwined with everyday life rather than restricted to one day of the week within the walls of a church building. This outlook shaped the behavior and practices of the sectarians and differentiated them from the "church people."

"Church people" were members of the Lutheran and Reformed congregations. The Reformed church was known as the "mother of sects" because, like the sects, its adherents held that theologian Martin Luther had not gone far enough in correcting the excesses of the Catholic church. The Reformed thought too much pomp still remained in the Lutheran service and sought to encourage the laity to assist in church governance.

The Reformed church was not an official state religion in Germany, so its members often emigrated to avoid persecution; Lutherans left mostly for economic reasons. In Pennsylvania, however, the division between the two churches melted away as the population of German immigrants grew. Out of necessity Lutheran and Reformed congregations shared church buildings and ministers. Intermarriage between the two faiths became common.

Of course, some immigrants did not belong to any religion. In 1701, one minister bemoaned the unchurched condition of many of his fellow immigrants, "perhaps the majority, who despise God's word and all outward good order; who blaspheme the sacraments, and frightfully and publicly give scandal." The rough and tumble atmosphere of a booming port and colony did not encourage spiritual purity.

German peasants sought the chance to own land, or at least to work, in America. Although conditions in the new land were sometimes harsh, economic opportunities were generally better than in the old.

The Perils of the Port

In the mid-18th century, the port of arrival still favored by Germans was Philadelphia. The firm base of Germans who had already settled there and the glowing accounts of Pennsylvania that reached those back home through letters, brochures, and pamphlets assured its reputation. So did an increasingly well-established "triangle" of trade with corners at London, Rotterdam, and Philadelphia. From 1727, when arrivals in Philadelphia began to be officially recorded, immigration to that port increased yearly and steadily. The peak years were 1749–54, when more than 37,000 German immigrants arrived there.

Some of those who arrived in this boom period were dismayed by the gap between what was advertised and what they found. As early as 1728 a nameless diarist raged against those who had deluded him: "O these Liars! who in their well-written and printed missives send us such glowing accounts. . . . If I had but wings to fly, I would soon hie myself from hence to Europe, but I dread the impestuous ocean and the pirates."

If an immigrant was lucky enough to escape such disasters, he or she still had to contend with cramped quarters, lice, and the ship's fare, which according to the above diarist "consisted of horrible salted corned pork, peas, barley, groats, and codfish. The drink was a stinking water, in which all food was cooked." This description actually seems relatively mild in comparison with Gottfried Mittelberger's account of 1750, when abuses by profit-seeking merchants were at their height:

> The water which is served out on the ships is often very black, thick, and full of worms. . . . Towards the end we were compelled to eat the ship's biscuit which had been spoiled long ago . . . though in a whole biscuit there was scarcely a piece the size of a dollar that had not been full of red worms and spider's nests.

The nameless diarist of 1728 concludes that the trip should be made only by "poor and industrious persons, whose life in Europe had become unbearable, and [who] were willing to risk the voyage as a matter of life or death."

Those without money were not without recourse. Shippers willingly extended credit to passengers in order to fill their holds with emigrants. Under what was called the *redemption* system, passengers could either pay a portion of their fare ahead of time (the remainder to be paid by relatives or friends upon arrival) or "redeem" their fare in labor once the ship docked in Philadelphia.

As soon as a ship carrying redemptioners arrived in port, a doctor arrived to determine whether anyone carried a contagious disease. Healthy immigrants were then taken as a group to a land office to swear an oath of allegiance to the king of Britain. They then returned to the ship until word was spread that they had arrived and their labor was available.

Interested citizens would board the ship in search of someone who suited their needs. After paying the ships' captain or agent, the new master and servant would make their way to a government office where the immigrant signed over his or her labor for a specified amount of time. "Young persons" were usually signed up immediately because they were strong and obliged to serve apprenticeships until they turned 21, but the old and feeble were sometimes passed over and had to rely on the charity of established settlers in order to find a position and a place to live. Families sometimes had teenage members serve extra time for those who were too weak or elderly to work off the cost of passage.

After 1750 nearly half of all arriving immigrants were redemptioners, though even before it became a common practice young people would voluntarily indenture themselves (contract their labor for a given period of time) to a citizen. They did so either to learn a trade or to secure themselves financially before they set out on their own. One young redemptioner whose journey began in Rotterdam was apprenticed in 1771 to a Philadelphia house carpenter. The boy agreed to serve for five years, and the master agreed to teach him "the art, trade, and mystery of a house carpenter," as well as "the first five rules in common arithmetic" in two winters of schooling.

Although some redemptioners profited from their terms of indenture and even esteemed their masters, no one in retrospect admired the *newlanders*, men hired by the shipping companies to fill up the ships. Promised a commission for each passenger they secured, newlanders would tell almost any story or use any method to persuade prospective emigrants to book passage. They earned their name through a common ploy: Dressed in sumptuous clothing and brandishing gold watches and other valuables, they told awe-inspiring stories of the abundance of wealth in the "new land."

Mittelberger called these agents "men-thieves" and described some of the tricks they pulled, from one who convinced a wealthy widow to hand over her money for safekeeping and then stole it, to others who forged letters they claimed were written by relatives in America. Mittelberger told how he, on his return home, was nearly convinced by some newlanders in Rotterdam that he should board the next ship back to America

Swindlers of all kinds preyed upon travelers at both ends of their voyage. "Newlanders" in Germany touted the wonders of the "new land" in order to fill their employers' boats with emigrants, and labor agents on the other end bought the services of the new arrivals.

By the 1750s, German immigrants lived in each of the 13 colonies. This view, near Morristown, New Jersey, shows the much-praised orderliness of the farms they established.

when they showed him a letter from his wife saying that she had taken their son to meet him in Pennsylvania. Fortunately, he suspected a forgery and made the trip back up the Rhine to find his wife and son where he had left them.

Many unlucky emigrants fell prey to other kinds of abuse: 36 toll stations on the Rhine between Strassbourg and Rotterdam; the long and costly wait in Rotterdam for a crossing to London; the loss or theft of their belongings. To make more room on ship, captains often separated the passengers from their trunks, many of which never reached the port of arrival.

The lucrative transportation of German immigrants came to an end during the Seven Years' War (1756–63) (in North America called the French and Indian Wars, 1754–63), when Great Britain won command of the seas. By then, however, more than 240 ships carrying German immigrants had docked in Philadelphia. Many people had died in transit, but the German population in Pennsylvania had still grown so large that in 1747, Governor George Thomas estimated that they formed three-fifths of the state's total population of 200,000. Moreover, in a letter to the Bishop of Exeter in England, Thomas praised the contributions of the Germans: "They have, by their industry, been the principal instruments of raising the state to its present flourishing condition, beyond any of his Majesty's Colonies, in North America."

Anti-German feeling did exist; it was far from a powerful force, however. Even men like Benjamin Franklin, who described German immigrants in a 1753 letter as "Palatine boors" and "generally the most stupid of their own nation," were rarely entirely hostile. Franklin himself supported the founding of a college to teach English to the Germans in Pennsylvania and was a key player in the successful attempt to obtain a generalship in the American revolutionary army for German immigrant Baron Friedrich von Steuben.

By the 1750s, there were Germans in each of the 13 colonies. By 1770 there were between 225,000 and 250,000 of them in America. Almost three-quarters of

Persecuted Lutherans from Salzburg (now in Austria), depart for Georgia in 1732. Only a few hundred German settlers headed for the southern American colonies. Many objected to slavery on religious grounds, but more often they stayed away because a free laborer with few skills could not compete in the slave economy.

the German immigrants ended up in the middle colonies—New York, New Jersey, and Pennsylvania—the last of which remained their center of settlement. Some 20 percent could be found in the southern colonies—Maryland, Virginia, the Carolinas, and Georgia.

There were reasons for Germans to avoid other regions. New England, for example, was largely made up of Puritans who did not tolerate religious dissenters, especially the sectarians so numerous in Pennsylvania. Moreover, because New England was one of the first areas of the country to be settled, farmland was scarce, and in any case it was less fruitful than the limestone land German farmers found in the middle colonies.

In the South, another firmly established tradition deterred German settlers—the plantation system and slave ownership. Germans in America generally did not own slaves, and sectarians in particular openly objected to the practice. Francis Pastorius and a group of Dutch and German Quakers reportedly made the first official protest against slavery in America in a 1688 letter to the Quaker Meeting in Philadelphia. Nothing much came of the protest; it was quietly shelved. One story—or legend—tells of a Mennonite farmer who refused to stay with a friend when he witnessed the ill treatment of one of the man's slaves. Instead of entering the man's house, the Mennonite slept in a nearby field. Such moral objections aside, the chief reason that Germans avoided the South was probably their realization that free labor could not compete with the slave labor established there.

The Lure of the Land

Nonetheless, Germans settled throughout the colonies, sometimes migrating within the colonies as well. The largest single emigration of the colonial period, the exodus of 1709, was sparked by recurring attacks on the Palatinate by French armies. More than 13,000 refugees from the regions along the Main, Neckar, and Rhine rivers arrived that year in London, where they aroused resentment and fear of disease. Queen Anne, a Protestant, ordered the Roman Catholics among them sent back to Holland, and about 3,000 others, mostly linen weavers, were sent to Ireland. A group of 650 settlers were sent to North Carolina, where they settled in New Bern, a community that fell under attack by Tuscarora Indians only a year after its founding. Under a plan devised by the queen and the governor of New York, 2,814 of the refugees were sent to the Hudson Valley area to manufacture tar and turpentine and to protect the frontier from Indians.

The voyage from London to New York took six months, and about one-quarter of the Palatines did not survive the journey. Nor did adequate preparations await them in New York—they were housed in tents, and some of the children were advertised as orphans and parceled off as apprentices. At this point Queen Anne granted them land of their own, but before they could claim it a landlord named Robert Livingstone moved a

Reports in the 18th and 19th centuries of the bountiful lands of North America inspired idealized engravings such as this. Game, fish, and fowl were said to exist in limitless supply.

The so-called Pennsylvania Dutch, actually Germans, took both whimsical and functional crafts with them as they dispersed into new counties and states. This pie plate depicts colonial soldiers at a dance.

large number of the Germans to a tract of his land, putting the men to work burning tar and cultivating hemp "to defray the expenses incurred by Queen Anne." In addition, Livingstone charged them rent and even passage money.

One of the immigrants so compromised was John Conrad Weiser, who in 1713 led an unsuccessful resistance movement. The next spring, 150 families left Livingstone's settlements for Schoharie, 40 miles from Albany. Weiser's son noted that they "broke ground enough to plant corn for their own use the next year. But this year our hunger was hardly endurable." Conditions improved slowly, and within a few years they had their own grist mill.

Just as the Germans had established this community, a group of seven landlords, including Livingstone, claimed ownership of it. They demanded rent, which the Germans refused to pay. Weiser and two others went to England to appeal to Queen Anne but found upon their arrival that she had died and that the landlords had sent their own representative, "who knew but too well how to misrepresent the Germans as rebels, as a pestiferous set and as enemies to the crown," wrote Weiser. The Germans landed in debtor's prison until they were rescued with funds sent from home. In 1723, Weiser returned to America and, along with the majority of the settlers, left Schoharie soon thereafter. Some 60 families eventually settled with him in Berks County, Pennsylvania.

Not all the Germans who arrived in New York in 1710 wound up on Livingstone's land; many of the original German settlers of New Jersey belonged to this group of immigrants. Other Germans moved from Pennsylvania to New Jersey to settle along the Raritan River. Moravians (a sect of evangelical Protestants) from Bethlehem, Pennsylvania, established a settlement named Hope on this river, on land they had purchased from two converts. William Whipple, a signer of the Declaration of Independence, passed through Hope in 1776 and described "five or six private houses, some mechanics' shops, a merchant's store and one of the finest and most curious mills in America. All the Moravian buildings are strong, neat, and compact and very generally made of stone." Nevertheless, Hope dissolved in 1808 and the property was sold.

Spanning the Colonies

Despite the concentration of Germans in the middle colonies, there were small German enclaves in the South and New England. Sometimes these were the results of efforts by landowners and colonizers seeking to populate their large tracts of land. In Louisiana, for example, a Scottish financier named John Law established "La Compagnie des Indes" in 1717. In exchange for a 25-year trade monopoly and control of the land, Law's company promised the French crown (who then owned the land) to bring in 9,000 people (6,000 whites and 3,000 blacks) who would introduce agriculture to the swampy, uncultivated region along the Mississippi and Arkansas rivers. Until this time, New Orleans had been a dumping ground for "undesirable" French citizens (thieves, prostitutes, and freed prisoners), and Law resolved to recruit German farmers who, he believed, could help him fulfill his part of the bargain. The recruiting effort that followed was echoed by other landowners in other parts of the country who sought settlers for their unpopulated lands. Law published a pamphlet enticing hundreds of Germans to cross the ocean; once they came, however, he treated them poorly. Yet the Germans remained to settle what came to be known as the German Coast of Louisiana.

Other settlements in the South were established as the result of religious persecution. Ebenezer, Georgia, was founded by a group of Salzburgers whose motto was "Hitherto hath the Lord helped us." They had been exiled by a 1731 decree of Archbishop Leopold of Salzburg (in present-day Austria), who, to appease the pope, promised that he would rid his diocese of all Protestants.

South Carolina and North Carolina came by their German populations differently. Those in South Carolina arrived directly from Europe, through the port of Charleston. In North Carolina, as in other colonies, the Germans settled largely on the frontier, in the rural regions that spread out behind the port cities. In 1735, subjects of the Prince of Orange founded Orangeburg, in the first inland county colonized in the state. From this district, the Germans spread into Saxe-Gotha (now Lexington County), and from there into the counties of Richland and Fairfield, whose names were chosen in praise of the land itself.

Germans began arriving in the highlands of Virginia in 1745, as part of a more general movement out of Pennsylvania into the surrounding colonies. Land in Pennsylvania had become scarce; it could be bought from the Indians only in small parcels along the frontier. Even this land was soon difficult to purchase, despite the dangerous living conditions there. In 1732, a Pennsylvania German named Jost Hite led 16 families across the Potomac River and into the Shenandoah Valley in Virginia, where they settled near Winchester. Other German settlers founded Strasburg, Woodstock, and Shepherdstown, Virginia. In fact, the portion of the Shenandoah Valley sloping to the north was almost entirely settled by Germans from Pennsylvania.

These travelers to Virginia passed over the Monocacy Road, an old Indian trail named after a river in Maryland. Because the colony of Maryland was the private holding of a Catholic, Lord Baltimore, most German immigrants (who were predominantly Protestant) had not considered it a good place for settlement. Lord Baltimore, however, noticed the streams of immigrants headed for Virginia and offered the Germans especially agreeable terms for settlement: Any family arriving within 3 years of March 1732 in the "backlands" of Maryland would receive a 200-acre tract of land free of charge for the first 3 years; thereafter rent would be only 1 cent per acre per year. Moreover, Lord Baltimore vowed that all settlers would be "as well secured in their liberty and property in Maryland as any of His Majesty's Subjects."

Most agricultural trade in Maryland had been in tobacco (an early 18th-century traveler reported that "Tobacco is their Meat, Drink, Clothing and Money"), but the German farmers passed over this crop in favor of grain production. As early as 1740, a road was built connecting Annapolis and the back counties on the Monocacy River and Conococheague Creek. Grain could be transported via these waterways to Baltimore for export.

Frederick County, encompassing western Maryland's best farmland, soon became dotted with tracts rented and named by Pennsylvanian Germans: "Bachelor's Delight," "I Wish There Was More," "Struggle," and "Hager's Defence." The last belonged to Jonathan Hager, who joined the land with "Hager's Delight" in 1762 to form Hagerstown, Maryland. Hager became the first German from western Maryland to be active in politics when he was elected to the General Assembly in 1771, but he was unable to take his seat because of an existing law barring naturalized citizens from holding office. The resulting uproar led the General Assembly to quickly overturn the law, and Hager regained his office in the next election.

The only large German group settlement in colonial New England was the community at Waldoboro, Maine (then a part of the colony of Massachusetts). In the 1740s, 300 mostly Lutheran natives of the Palatine and Württemberg agreed to come to Maine when promised land, a minister, a church, two large houses for their first winter, and the proprietor's support for a year after their arrival. They would settle on the large tract of land that Samuel Waldo, a prosperous Boston merchant (himself half-German), owned in the sparsely settled North.

The immigrants were met in Boston and escorted to their new home, then were left to fend for themselves. They passed their first winter in crude log cabins, subsisting chiefly on a broth made from rye. Their isolation made them particularly vulnerable to attacks from Cana-

Because much of the colony of Maryland was the private holding of a Catholic lord, Germans at first bypassed it. In 1732, however, they began to farm the state's fertile western reaches, where one newcomer established Hagerstown in 1762.

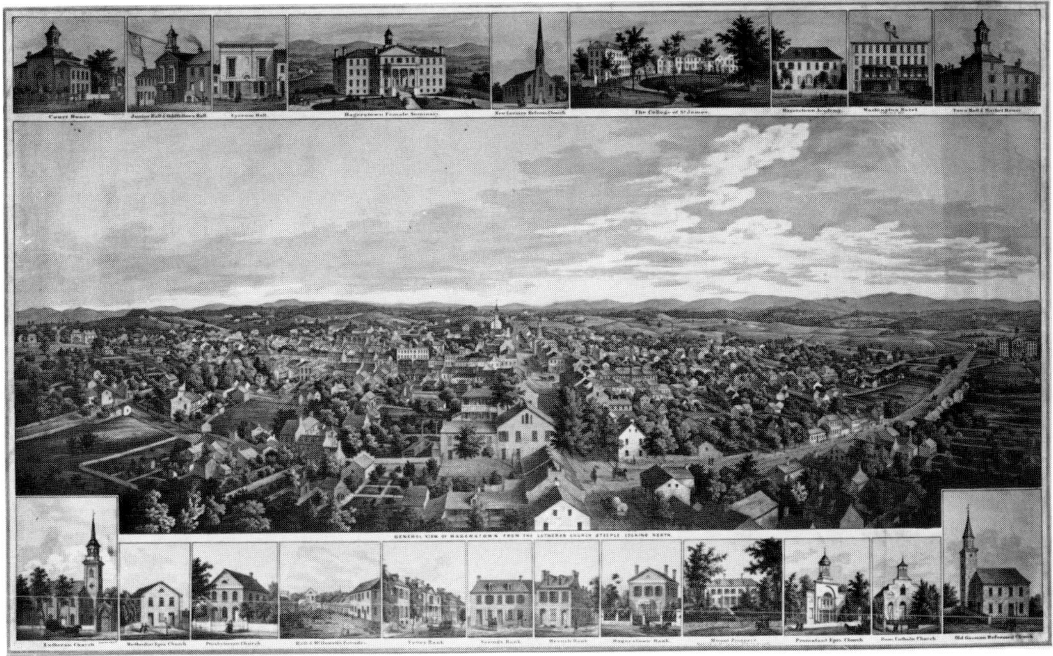

dian Indians. Some families fled to Nova Scotia, and those who remained were killed or captured. The settlement was all but deserted when, in 1752, it was strengthened by another group of Germans. They founded the town of Frankfurt on the Kennebec, followed by Dresden, into which Frankfurt was eventually incorporated.

After Waldo died suddenly in 1759, the extent of his legal holdings was called into question, and 300 people, disgusted with the news that they might have to repurchase their land from its rightful owners, left for the Carolinas.

The Revolution: A New Beginning

Though German settlers stood up for their rights as tenants or landowners and within their communities took leadership positions and mediated disputes, rare was the person who, like Jonathan Hager, was politically active on a grander scale. One theory to account for this is that they were grateful to have found freedom and peace in the New World and preferred not to stir up trouble. Another theory is that German settlers were usually agriculturalists and therefore isolated from towns and hence from the political process. A third issue was naturalization—it was not always easy for a German immigrant to become a citizen, and the right to vote was on occasion hard won.

It took the revolutionary war to propel the group into active involvement in the political life of the nation. Most Germans readily backed the cause of the revolutionaries, for they had felt the same rancor as most colonists at the British acts that were the immediate cause of war. The 1765 Stamp Act, for example, which required all official transactions to be printed on paper stamped by the government, aroused widespread resentment. German citizens in Frederick, Maryland, burned an effigy of the new stamp collector; when a local court struck down the Stamp Act, they celebrated with a parade. (Because they did not drink tea, German immigrants were not particularly affected by the tea tax.) Another law that angered them required all citi-

zens to pay a tax to the local Anglican (Church of England) diocese. For Lutherans and Calvinists, who had left Europe to escape exactly that type of religious and economic oppression, the law seemed unjust.

Most Lutheran and Reformed ministers offered the revolutionaries enthusiastic support. Some sects believed in pacifism and aroused suspicion among the general population, but on the whole, even these sectarians were supportive. If they did not fight, they supplied grain from the "breadbasket of America" and munitions from the regions of Pittsburgh and western Maryland. Artisans contributed shoes, stockings, and paper for the cartridge wrappings. The Kentucky rifles the colonials carried were often fashioned by Pennsylvania-German gunsmiths. A British soldier wrote in 1775 that these "cursed twisted guns [were] the most fatal widow-orphan-makers in the world."

Some German immigrants supported the British, and large numbers of men from Hesse-Kassel and several other German states were sold by their princes and forced to serve in the British army. More than 30,000 mercenaries, known as Hessians, no matter which state

In this mural from 1896, painted for the capitol in Harrisburg, Pennsylvania, Baron Friedrich Wilhelm von Steuben, a German nobleman, drills General George Washington's troops at Valley Forge, Pennsylvania. Von Steuben spearheaded the organization of the Continental army; he later became an American citizen.

Both as farmers feeding the troops and as artisans providing well-made guns, Germans supported the revolutionary cause.

they originally came from, were sent to America during the course of the war, though many Hessians deserted to join the American cause. In fact, it was an American policy to print broadsides in German to encourage desertion. Hessians who were taken prisoner were often treated exceptionally well. One officer, Andreas Wiederholdt, was captured at the Battle of Trenton (December 26, 1776) and was eventually taken to Fredericksburg, Virginia. His diary records that

> the residents are the friendliest and most courteous in America no matter what their standings and their opinion. Tories and [Whigs] are hospitable and obliging to everyone, especially strangers. The women are pretty, courteous, friendly and modest . . . ; we enjoyed a great deal of civility from them and not-with-standing the fact that we are enemies, they gave us a great preference over their own men at balls and other occasions.

Wiederholdt and his fellow officers had petitioned Congress to send them to Fredericksburg from the

Shenandoah Valley of Virginia, where, apparently, they had encountered a great deal of hostility from German residents.

But elsewhere the Hessians were welcomed by German settlers. Prisoners of war were sent to Frederick, Maryland, and many worked with local farmers and became part of the community. In all, more than 6,000 Hessians remained in America after the war ended. Then it was their musical talents that were of particular use: When word came to Frederick in March 1783 that the war had ended, a Hessian officer and his band played at the victory ball there.

An array of political, religious, and historical factors gave German immigrants social and economic security in the new land—and industriousness and group effort had something to do with it, too. As the largest non-English element in colonial America, perhaps they were also eager to make the switch from being Germans in a British colony to being Americans. Their success paved the way for thousands of their countrymen to follow.

Emigrants leave Basel, Switzerland, for America, in May 1805. The exodus from German-speaking lands would eventually take more than 5 million Germans and Swiss to America in the 19th century.

SETTLING THE NEW NATION

The American Revolution, the Napoleonic Wars in Europe (1801–15), and the War of 1812 all discouraged emigration to the New World. Instead, the first 40 years of the American republic were years of assimilation rather than expansion for the German-American population. Still, immigrants trickled in. In 1804, a group of separatists from Württemberg founded Harmony, Pennsylvania. Like many of their 18th-century forerunners, these settlers—known as Rappists after their leader, George Rapp—sought to live by the Scriptures. They practiced celibacy, and residents signed over all personal wealth to create their "Community of Goods." In 1814, the Rappists moved to Indiana, where they established New Harmony on 30,000 acres, but "to avoid malaria and bad neighbors" they headed back to Pennsylvania 10 years later. Their final home was Economy, on the Ohio River, 20 miles north of Pittsburgh. Here, finally, they found prosperity—oil wells, coal mines, and numerous factories sprang up by the 1820s.

Other American communities founded by religious Germans and run—often very successfully—on the principle of common ownership of property cropped up later: Zoar, Ohio, in 1819; Bethel, Missouri, in 1844; Aurora, Oregon, and Amana, Iowa, in 1856. But by and large, the emigrant leaving his home for religious reasons

Bethlehem, Pennsylvania, was founded by German Moravians. An English American once called their buildings "strong, neat, and compact." The town's Moravians still host a choral festival each year.

was a rarity in the 19th century. A Württemberg government survey found that among those leaving the state in 1817, almost 90 percent left "to overcome famine, shrinking means, and unfavorable prospects." This was reflected in the makeup of the emigrant groups: while in the 18th century entire communities left Germany together, in the 19th century almost all emigrants traveled as individuals or in small family groups. Not all chose America; two-thirds of the emigrants set out for Austria-Hungary or for Russia. During the 1820s, only 6,000 to 8,000 Germans reached the United States.

By the end of the decade, several factors were encouraging German emigration. Overpopulation and a shortage of cash for trade, combined with the traditional practice of *Realteilungsbrecht*—the division of the family farm among many descendants—created enormous economic pressures. Many families had coped with shrinking farmlands by taking up handicrafts such as clockmaking or weaving, but after the end of the Napoleonic Wars Germany was flooded with cheap factory-made English goods that brought disaster to German family industries. The appearance of Gottfried Duden's book *Report on a Journey to the Western States of North America* in 1829, thus was timely. His account of life on a small farm in Missouri sounded idyllic to those who saw their way of life fast slipping away from them.

Next Stop: Missouri

With a population of about 70,000, Missouri became a state in 1821. Duden purchased 270 acres of land in present-day Warren County, Missouri, in 1824 and he was soon convinced that planned farm communities of Germans were feasible. "No plan in this age," he wrote, "can promise more for the individual or group."

The careful advice he gave was less compelling than his descriptions of daily life. Duden spent the hour before breakfast "shooting partridges, pigeons, or squirrels, and also turkeys," and the rest of the day unfolded in a leisurely fashion: he read, strolled in his garden, visited neighbors, and "delight[ed] in the beauties of nature." His assurances that the educated man could make a go of it on the American frontier fed the imaginations of many young liberals in Germany, intellectuals disgusted with the reactionary policies the German states adopted after the Napoleonic Wars.

The Giessen Emigration Society, founded in 1833, was the first of many such organized emigration movements to try to profit by the disenchantment in the old country. Their pamphlets, widely distributed in southwest Germany, urged readers to join them and help found "a free German state, a rejuvenated Germany in North America." That state was never realized, as a group of about 500 emigrants under the society's auspices disbanded upon reaching St. Louis.

Many of the Giesseners were dubbed "Latin Farmers" because of their classical education. They soon dis-

Karl Pflaume's farm in Wisconsin, 1855. Pflaume was one of the many "Latin farmers" from Germany whose classical education left them better prepared for philosophy than farming. German immigrants of this era branched out across the Midwest, often starting from St. Louis.

covered that pioneer farming was not as leisurely as Duden had described. Karl Buchele, in an 1855 book, summarized their predicament: "The German philosopher who . . . has here become a farmer, finds that the American axe is more difficult to wield than the pen, and that the plow and the manure-fork are very matter-of-fact and stupid tools." Another disgruntled immigrant labeled Duden a *Lugenhund* (lying dog), and Duden felt compelled to retract some of his own advice in an 1837 sequel to his 1829 book.

In the time between the two books, however, more than 50,000 Germans emigrated, many of them at Duden's suggestion. Many came from areas of Germany—Hannover and Oldenburg, for example—that had previously lost few citizens. The Latin Farmers formed the vanguard of German settlement in Missouri, and they quickly spread into southern Illinois. In spite of all gloomy predictions, they came to be an important local influence, establishing libraries, schools, and newspapers.

A colonization attempt inspired by the Giessener Society later in the decade proved even more successful. In 1837, the German Philadelphia Settlement Society bought about 12,000 acres in Gasconade County, across the river from Duden's land, then dispatched an advance party of 17 to spend the winter on the property. This group was joined by a steadily increasing flow of members from back east, and by 1839, when it was incorporated, Hermann, Missouri, boasted 450 inhabitants, 90 houses, 5 stores, 2 inns, and a post office. The society dissolved in 1840, but Hermann and the surrounding district gave rise to a prosperous fruit-growing and wine-producing industry. In this "Little Germany," wrote a visitor, "one forgets that one is not actually in Germany itself."

The Taming of Texas

As German immigration accelerated in the 1840s (tripling from the 125,000 arrivals of the previous decade),

(continued on page 57)

FOLK ARTS, FINE ART

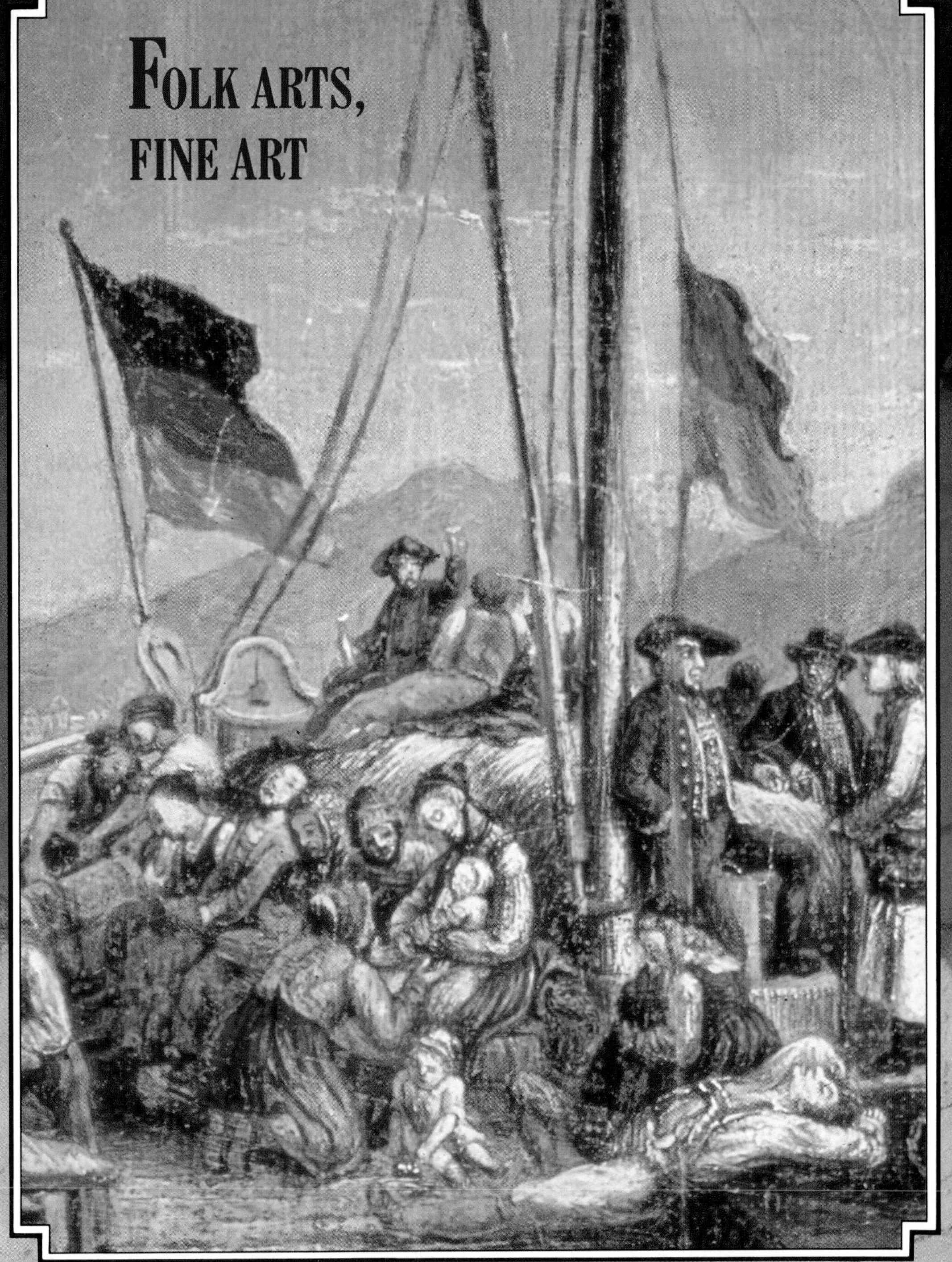

(Overleaf) Emigrants on the Rhine, *painted by an anonymous artist in 1863. Until about 1830, most Germans bound for the Western Hemisphere sailed down the Rhine from southwest Germany to Dutch seaports. Once transatlantic steamers in the mid-19th century shortened the voyage, and as word about America's promise spread to other parts of Germany, emigration gathered force.*

(Right) Pennsylvania Lady, *probably by Jacob Maentel, about 1815–20.*

Auswand'rers Freud' in Amerika:
Auswand'rers Leid in Amerika.

A two-panel caricature (above) from the 1840s makes sport of the wayfarers' dreams about the New World. The first panel, Emigrant's Joys in America, *depicts a typical immigrant fantasy: adventurers enjoying the fruits of the land. The second panel,* Emigrant's Sufferings in America, *shows the real conditions—backbreaking labor, rutted land, and a blazing sun. (Right)* The Crucifixion, *by an anonymous folk artist, helped illustrate a religious book published in 1847.*

Floreat Commercium
Charles Ghequiere

Christlicher Haus-Seegen,

Nebst den

Zwölf Stunden Gedächtniß.

Haus Seegen.

*Arts for the home: (Left) A Christian House Blessing (*Haus-Segen*) written in Gothic script with watercolor and ink by a German-American monk who lived in Pennsylvania during and after the revolutionary war. (Far left) In the 18th century, German Americans expanded the glass industry with striking objects such as this covered tumbler, produced in 1788 by John Frederick Amelung's glassworks, located in New Bremen, Maryland. (Below) A dower chest of 1794, made in Pennsylvania, combines Old World patterns with elements, such as flowers, observed in the new land.*

Albert Bierstadt (1830–1902) was born in Germany and came to the United States as a child. The landscapes of both countries excited his imagination. In this 1850 canvas, Among the Sierra Nevadas, *the California range resembles the sharply peaked crests of the Bavarian Alps. Bierstadt depicted the Far West in other landscapes and also in historical scenes showing America's frontier expansion. But he remains best known as a member of the Hudson River school of painters whose canvases paid homage to the New York river valley often likened to Germany's Rhineland.*

Fourth of July in Centre Square, *painted in 1819 by German-American John Lewis Krimmel, offers a glimpse of the festivities held in Philadelphia, where an assortment of ethnic Americans—including Germans, English, and Irish—joined to celebrate the independence of their chosen homeland.*

(continued from page 48)
the desire to bolster cultural and economic ties with the New World became popular in Germany. Yet colonization proved no easier than it had been in the 1830s. All over Germany, local societies to aid the emigrant sprang up, but without a unified central government the region could not promote the concerted settlement that such countries as France and England managed. Independent attempts—like that of the Giessener Society—tended instead to open up areas for subsequent immigrants who acted on their own.

Such was the case in Texas. An independent republic from 1836 to 1845, Texas was a likelier prospect than midwestern states for colonization schemes. The Germania Society of New York, founded in 1838, chose Texas because "the plan of founding a pure German state in the midst of the American Union would arouse the opposition of the American people." An outbreak of fever among settlers in Galveston in 1838, however, forced the society to abort its plans.

News of Texas had reached the northeastern states of Germany by way of a letter sent in 1832 by immigrant Friedrich Ernst to a friend in Oldenburg praising the land and life in Texas. Published first in an Oldenburg newspaper and then in a book on Texas, the letter induced the first wave of German immigrants—mostly from the states of Oldenburg, Westphalia, and Holstein—to emigrate to Texas. One man whose imagination was captured by Ernst's letter wrote that it depicted a beautiful landscape "with enchanting scenery and delightful climate similar to that of Italy" and "the most fruitful soil and republican government." These attractions enticed settlers much like those who had responded to Gottfried Duden's descriptions of Missouri. Like the Latin Farmers, some of these newcomers were disillusioned upon their arrival. One immigrant, Rosa von Roeder Kleberg, wrote, "My brothers had pictured pioneer life as one of hunting and fishing, of freedom from the restraints of Prussian society; and it was hard for them to settle down to the drudgery and toil of splitting rails and cultivating the field, work which was entirely new to them."

Between 1831 and Ernst's arrival, Germans continued to go to Texas, but compared to the influx of Germans into Missouri, Texan settlement was slight. In 1836, the total number of Germans barely exceeded 200. Texas seemed too remote to most immigrants. It was also vulnerable to attack by Comanche Indians from the west.

Nevertheless, in 1843 the republic was chosen for a colonization project known as the *Adelsverein* (nobles club). Composed of 24 rulers and nobles, the Germania Society aimed, "out of purely philanthropical reasons," to "devote itself to the support and direction of German emigration to Texas." No doubt Prince Carl of Solms-Braunfels, the commissioner general of the project, envisioned other, more glorious objectives when he wrote that "the eyes of all Europe are fixed on us and our undertaking."

The society's prospectus detailed the terms of the "new Fatherland beyond the Seas." For the equivalent

Mr. and Mrs. August Krueger cradle and rake grain on their fields in Dodge County, Wisconsin, about 1900. Starting in the 1830s, economic hardship created by poor harvests and tight money spurred tens of thousands of Germans to emigrate annually, many of them settling in the undeveloped reaches of the Midwest.

of $120, a person received free passage and 40 acres in west-central Texas. From December 1844 (when the first 3 shiploads of immigrants landed at Carlshafen, later renamed Indianola) to 1847 (when the society went bankrupt), more than 7,000 Germans were transported to Texas under the auspices of the Adelsverein. Prince Carl von Solms-Braunfels proved to be an incompetent leader, preoccupied with decorum rather than the nuts and bolts of founding a town. He built a stockade, called Sophienburg in honor of his lady, and manned it with a courtly company of soldiers. He did, however, with 180 subscribers, found the town of New Braunfels in 1845. This settlement, wrote one American visitor, was an eventual success, "in spite of the Prince, who appears to have been an amiable fool, aping, among the log-cabins, the nonsense of medieval courts."

In 1845, the prince was replaced as commissioner general, but adversity dogged the immigrants. Comanches threatened attack; the United States had begun its war with Mexico over the annexation of Texas; and the society was debt ridden. One thousand of the settlers died in squalid camps on the coast.

Those who survived were encouraged to spread out over new land northwest of New Braunfels. Particularly notable was the founding of Fredericksburg in April 1846. Named in honor of Prince Frederick of Prussia, it was the first white settlement in the northwest hill country of Texas, and by 1850 it had a population of nearly 2,000. An enthusiastic inhabitant wrote to a friend:

> If you work only half as much as in Germany, you can live without troubles. In every sense of the word, we are *free*. The Indians do us no harm; on the contrary, they bring us meat and horses to buy. We still live so remote from other people that we are lonely, but we have dances, churches, and schools.

Such letters spurred further emigration to Texas, unmanaged by any colonization society. Estimates of

In the 1840s Texas caught on among Germans seeking a "new Fatherland beyond the Seas," in the words of Carl, prince of Solms-Braunfels. The prince's decorous ways proved no match for the rigors of leading a 7,000-person colony, but the town of New Braunfels held on, and Germans established themselves widely in the state.

the number of Germans who settled in Texas before the Civil War reach as high as 30,000. In 1857, a New Orleans editor wrote that every ship leaving from that port for Galveston was "crowded with Germans of some wealth . . . going to select a future home." The area of heaviest German concentration stretched from Galveston northwest to Austin, New Braunfels, and Fredericksburg.

In Texas, as in Missouri (and later, Wisconsin), the idea of a "new Germany" was never realized. The idea did, however, encourage settlement in rural, undeveloped areas of the country. And a large proportion of Germans arriving in the United States in the period from 1830 to 1860 looked as well to a different kind of destination for a new life: the growing cities of the Midwest.

Growing with the Cities

There was a variety of reasons for heavy German settlement in midwestern cities during the 19th century. For the lower-middle-class immigrants of the earlier period (1830–45), Cincinnati, Ohio; St. Louis, Missouri; and Milwaukee, Wisconsin, offered the skilled craftsmen many opportunities for employment in agriculturally related occupations (brewing, tanning, and milling). To farmers, cities offered a stopover, a place to earn enough money to buy land in the surrounding countryside. St. Louis also became the home for those cultured Germans who had tried, and then abandoned, the difficult life of the pioneer farmer. After 1845, with the incoming German population composed more and more of people with little means and few skills, laborers were drawn to the Midwest by the promise of plentiful employment in fields such as construction and transportation. One writer gave this advice: "Lose no time . . . in working your way out of New York and directing your steps westward, where labor is plentiful and sure to meet with its reward."

Travel routes, westward from New York or north from New Orleans, played a major role in determining

the destination of many 19th-century immigrants. Natural and man-made waterways were the "highways" of the 1830s and 1840s. The Erie Canal, opened in October 1825, was especially important, linking the Atlantic coast with the region beyond the Allegheny mountains. Arriving in New York (the busiest port of the mid-19th century), an immigrant could take a steamboat up the Hudson River to Albany; a week's trip from Albany on the Erie Canal landed him in Buffalo. From Buffalo, the Great Lakes provided access to Wisconsin, Michigan, Ohio, Indiana, Illinois, and Minnesota. The advent of the railroads made travel much easier—by 1851, an immigrant with some money to spare could cover the distance from New York to Lake Erie by train. Populations reflected this advance. Chicago in 1845 was eight percent German; by 1860, when it had become the hub of the flourishing rail system, Germans accounted for one-quarter of the city's total inhabitants.

Germans congregated in their own neighborhoods in Cincinnati (pictured here), where half of the city's population in 1850 was German, and in dozens of other middle-Atlantic and midwestern cities—Baltimore, Maryland; Louisville, Kentucky; Chicago, Illinois; and Milwaukee, Wisconsin, among others. They dominated the meat-packing and brewing industries for decades to come.

Chicago filched its status as the center of the Midwest from Cincinnati. Situated at the point where the Great and Little Miami rivers flow into the Ohio, Cincinnati was the boomtown of the 1830s, the era of the waterways. Germans contributed substantially to its growth: By 1841, 28 percent of the total population was German; 10 years earlier the figure was only 5 percent. By 1850, when Cincinnati was known as the "Queen City of the West," the German community (including those born in America) made up half its population.

From 1847 to 1855, a period of especially high European immigration because of poor harvests in the Old World, Germans flocked to Wisconsin. A state bureau of immigration, railroad companies, and eager immigrants themselves encouraged settlement in the new state, which entered the Union in 1848. One German-language newspaper sold stationery preprinted with a "brief but true" description of Wisconsin. Milwaukee, settled in 1836 where the Milwaukee River flows into Lake Michigan, attracted many of the newcomers. More than 8,000 Germans arrived there during the 1850s, and in 1860, Germans accounted for 16,000 out of a total population of 45,000.

Unlike the Irish, who also formed a substantial immigrant population in Milwaukee, Germans tended to flock together in their own neighborhoods. Likewise, in Cincinnati, the focus of the German community was an area known as "Over-the-Rhine," across the canal from the main part of town. St. Louis, however (where from 1830 to 1850 the population exploded from 7,000 to 77,860), did not boast an exclusively German neighborhood. Its German population—22,340 in 1850, and more than 50,000 just 10 years later—was spread throughout the city's 28 districts.

Jews also figured largely in the migration from Germany to the United States in these years. Between 1840 and 1880 the Jewish-American population grew from 15,000 to 250,000 persons, most of them Germans. Like their Christian contemporaries, they took their

Two German Catholics in Kansas, about 1875. After the mid-19th century, German Protestants were increasingly joined by German Catholics and German Jews in emigrating to America.

skills and culture primarily to midwestern cities, though the Jews tended to be merchants rather than artisans or laborers. A handful became highly successful owners of department stores; others, mostly in New York, built substantial houses of banking and finance, such as the Lehman, Kuhn, and Loeb families. Immigrant Levi Strauss, for instance, started a dry-goods store that became the blue jeans empire of today. The seeds of Reform Judaism, a modernization of some traditional Jewish practices and beliefs that is now the largest of Judaism's three main branches, also came from Germany with the immigrants and got its real start in America, led by Rabbi Isaac Mayer Wise in Cincinnati. The German Jews settled in tightly knit communities to better practice their faith—and because they were barred from many neighborhoods.

Differences in neighborhood arrangements from city to city raise a question about how German Christians or Jews and native-born Americans got along. Did the 19th-century German immigrants band together more than any group at any time, as one historian, John Hawgood, claimed? Or did they move into the mainstream of American life willingly and rapidly?

Settling In, Fitting In

The Germania Turnverein, a gymnastic club, Milwaukee, Wisconsin, 1892. Germans in America started or transplanted many athletic clubs, music and drama societies, church charities, and business associations. Their community spirit helped dispel some disparaging stereotypes.

The following comments, made by a visitor to a 19th-century midwestern German community, seem to support Hawgood's theory:

> Life in this settlement is only very slightly modified by the influence of the American environment. Different in language and customs, the Germans isolate themselves perhaps too much from the earlier settlers and live a life of their own, entirely shut off.

Although this observer was writing about a relatively secluded rural settlement in southern Illinois, urban life did not always foster rapid assimilation into an American way of life either. More than half a million people emigrated from Germany between 1852 and 1854 alone (many of them from areas in northern and eastern Germany previously unaffected by emigration). Sometimes a German immigrant felt a strong pressure to, in the words of one immigrant writer, "transform himself into a complete Yankee." But thanks to their large numbers, most Germans found it easy to preserve at least some distinctive elements of their culture.

Preservation of the mother tongue was of paramount importance in a person's battle to preserve ethnic identity. Even in St. Louis, bastion of the idealistic Germans of the recent immigration, the editors of a prominent German newspaper, the *Anzeiger des Westens*, mourned "the laming and corruption of the German language." A German-language school was established in St. Louis in 1836, two years before the city's public school opened. By 1860, there were 38 German schools in the city, most affiliated with Protestant and Catholic churches (though one was Jewish and one freethinking, or nonreligious). The very number of German children in these schools provided so much competition with the 35 public schools that in 1864 the local school board voted to include German-language instruction in the public school curriculum. There was one earlier exception to the rule of division by language: In 1850, John Kerler, Jr., stated that "Milwaukee is the only place in which I found that the Americans concern themselves with learning German, and where the German language and German ways are bold enough to take a foothold."

Nineteenth-century German immigrants often preserved their culture and language in their settlements. This German-Swiss woman, who arrived in 1831, lived 38 years in America without learning English.

Kerler described another attraction of Milwaukee—its "inns, beer cellars, and billiard and bowling alleys, as well as German beer." Indeed, by 1850 there were 7 German breweries in Milwaukee; a decade later there were 19, some with taverns or beer gardens where informal gatherings over German-style lager beer helped young men feel at home. Whole families also gathered there. In fact, in every major midwestern city, beer gardens like the Milwaukee Garden (established in 1850 and said to accommodate more than 12,000 patrons), took the place of public parks. Suburban "refreshment gardens" appeared on the outskirts of many midwestern towns.

Germans were also known for more formal social arrangements. The middle-class German immigrant brought to the urban and rural Midwest a tradition of forming and joining associations. These clubs, or *Vereine*, provided members both cultural and social nourishment, including drama, debate, and sharpshooter clubs. Many grew out of a love of music. The *Missouri Republican* observed that "the Germans best among all nations understand how to make music subservient to social enjoyment."

Gesangvereine, or German singing societies, were especially visible. Baltimore's *Liederkranz*, founded in 1836, stated its objective as "improvement in song and in social discourse through the same." The singing societies built concert halls, produced operas, and organized national choral festivals where groups from all over the country gathered to entertain huge audiences. One of America's greatest musical families started with Leopold Damrosch, a German immigrant of 1871 who founded an opera company. His son, Frank, was director of the Juilliard School of Music in New York City, and another son, Walter, was a conductor with the Metropolitan Opera Company and the New York Symphony Orchestra in the early 20th century.

Perhaps most characteristic of the German immigrants were the *Turnvereine*, or gymnastic clubs. Founded in Germany by Friedrich Jahn in 1811 as a means of promoting well-being through exercise, the clubs' programs also advocated nationalism and the need to defend the fatherland against Napoleon. In this sense, early Turnvereine were much like training camps. In America, "turners" still practiced gymnastics (the St. Louis school system enlisted the head of a local club to organize its physical education system), but they also arranged picnics, parades, and dances, serving a social as well as a sporting purpose. Some clubs took on the role of all-purpose community house in the 20th century. The Turnverein in Yorkville, New York City's largest German district, offered kindergarten classes to any neighborhood child before closing its doors in 1985. Others limited their offerings: The club in downtown Milwaukee became a German-style restaurant, its walls decorated with photographs of past gymnasts.

Churches set up their own brand of *Vereine*. Particularly common in Catholic parishes, these organizations ranged from mutual benefit associations (akin to insur-

Walter Damrosch was a leading orchestra conductor in the early 20th century. His father, German immigrant Leopold Damrosch, founded an opera company in New York City.

ance companies) to women's rosary and fund-raising societies. In Baltimore, a group called the Sisters of Charity was responsible for that city's first hospital, established in 1846. German Jews and Protestants also had their own associations.

The Forty-eighters

A particular boost to the sense of German ethnic identity came with the *forty-eighters*, a group of 4,000 to 10,000 Germans who arrived in America as refugees from the failed political revolutions and social-reform movements of 1848. On the whole they were liberal, agnostic, and intellectual, traits that threatened or offended many of the more established immigrants. But the influence of the forty-eighters on the cultural and political life of the German-American community was tremendous, and many worked to unite divergent groups of German Americans around issues that concerned Palatines and Berliners, Catholics and Protestants alike.

In the years immediately following their arrival, the forty-eighters continued to support, from across the ocean, the liberal cause in Germany. But troubling events in this country increasingly drew their attention. As early as 1835, antiforeign feelings had led to the establishment of the Know-Nothing party (so called because members continually claimed they "knew nothing" of the movement); by the early 1850s (coincidental with high mid-century immigration), the "nativism" favored by the Know-Nothings was on the rise. Nativists tried—through petition, legislation, ostracism, and open abuse—to restrict the entry of immigrants into the United States and to limit the rights of those who had already arrived.

One German custom especially appalling to native-born Americans was drinking beer on the Sabbath. Many native-born Americans followed the English Puritan tradition of refraining from frivolous activities such as dancing, bowling, and drinking on Sundays. Most German Americans had no such traditional restrictions

A 19th-century cartoon shows an Irish immigrant (identified with whiskey) and a German immigrant (identified with beer) stealing a ballot box during an election. Some native-born Americans felt threatened by the growing political power of such immigrants after the Civil War.

on Sabbath behavior, and their Sunday drinking caused such outrage that movements to restrict or prohibit liquor consumption arose in several states. Although most German immigrants agreed that moderation in drinking was a good idea, they viewed these legal efforts as direct attacks on both their way of life and their religious freedom. In Wisconsin (which by 1855 was heavily German), one newspaper lambasted "the Temperance Swindle" for reducing "all sociability to the condition of a Puritan graveyard." A German theater owner in St. Louis in 1861 defied a police order to close on Sunday, whereupon 40 officers arrived to prevent the audience from entering.

The culture gap had an uglier side. An 1855 riot in Louisville, Kentucky, led by the Know-Nothings, was one of the era's more blatant and violent manifestations of anti-German feeling. Catholics (both German and Irish) were frequently victims of attacks by nativists, who wanted a Protestant America. In the years immediately preceding the Civil War, opponents of slavery were also targets. Many of the more prominent German Americans, including most of the forty-eighters, spoke out against slavery, antagonizing slave owners and their sup-

The Ninth (German) Regiment of Ohio attacks with bayonets at the Battle of Somerset (Kentucky), 1862. When their patriotism was questioned during World War I, German Americans pointed to their sacrifices in the Civil War as evidence of their commitment to their new home.

porters. Most of these activists, moved by the strong antislavery stance of Republicans such as forty-eighter Carl Schurz, joined the Republican party soon after its founding in 1854. Although the average German immigrant did not own slaves, the Democratic party retained significant German-American support because it had formed the primary opposition to the Know-Nothing party in the past.

In general, German Americans felt more strongly about the preservation of the Union than about the abolition of slavery. By the time Republican Abraham Lincoln won the presidential election of 1860, seven southern states had already seceded from the Union, and German Americans (Republicans and Democrats alike) frowned upon this breach of national unity. After all, it was the search for economic and political stability that had motivated many of them to emigrate.

In December 1860, pro-Southern soldiers known as Minute Men resolved to further the cause of secession in the border state of Missouri. But the next May, federal troops thwarted their plans, capturing the pro-Southern state militia at Camp Jackson, near St. Louis. Many of the soldiers who stopped the Minute Men were German volunteers, members of *Turnvereine* or of Wide-Awake clubs (German organizations originally formed to protect Republican speakers at political rallies in Missouri). The result was that Missouri stayed in the Union, and German-American soldiers received much of the credit for the political victory.

Thousands of young German Americans—from Pennsylvania to Colorado—fought in the Civil War. Henry A. Kircher, 19, a first-generation American from Belleville, Illinois, left a record of his Civil War experiences in his letters home to his family. He initially joined the 9th Illinois Infantry but soon left, at least partially in response to ethnic tensions between Germans and Americans in that regiment. With a few other Germans from Belleville, he then joined the 12th Missouri Infantry, a regiment composed primarily of foreigners and led by German officers with such names as Osterhaus, Schadt, Wangelin, and Ledergreber.

In August 1864, after the Battle at Ringgold Gap (Georgia), Kircher's right arm and left leg were amputated; Captain Joseph Ledergreber died from shots through the lungs and spine. In sum, thousands of German Americans were injured or lost their life in battle. From the time the Civil War ended in April 1865 to well into the next century, German Americans pointed to these sacrifices for the Union as proof of their patriotism. For many, the Civil War would mark a turning point in their sense of themselves as American citizens.

An 1874 woodcut shows immigrants boarding ship in Hamburg, Germany. In the three decades following the Civil War, immigration to America boomed, with Germans still the most numerous of any ethnic group. These newcomers tended to be laborers, primarily from the northern and eastern states of the fatherland.

INDUSTRIALIZATION AND WAR

Two themes characterize German immigration in the decades between the Civil War and World War I. The first was a great increase in the number of new arrivals. The 1880s were the peak years of this exodus from the fatherland: In that decade, 1,445,181 Germans made their way across the Atlantic, about a quarter of a million of them in 1882 alone.

But a second, countervailing force was at work. In these same years, emigration from southern and eastern Europe began to climb, so that Germans fell sharply as a percentage of America's foreign-born population. Whereas in 1854 Germans accounted for about half of all foreign-born persons in America, by the 1890s that figure had fallen to less than one-fifth. Compared to the wave of Italians, Russian Jews, Scandinavians, Poles, and others, the Germans were in some senses part of the old America, a cultural presence that harked back to colonial times. These two facts changed the nature of the Germans' adaptation to their new homeland.

The source of German immigration was shifting, too. Whereas pre–Civil War immigrants hailed from the southwestern agricultural regions along the Rhine, the later arrivals were more likely to emigrate from the Hesses or Nassau. These northeastern states were dominated by estate agriculture, in which land was farmed commercially rather than by individual families. Consequently, a growing percentage of the emigrants were day laborers who had worked other people's fields, and who also, upon arriving in America, found most of the farmland occupied.

To the Frontier

The only area in North America still available for homesteading at this time was the Great Plains—the plateau stretching from Saskatchewan in Canada through the states of North Dakota, South Dakota, Nebraska, and Kansas. In the United States before 1875, this region was better known as the Great American Desert, a vast expanse to be suffered en route to more promising acreage in the Far West. Frequent skirmishes with Indians and the meager rainfall deterred most prospective farmers.

These conditions did not deter Russian Germans. Between 1872 and 1920, nearly 120,000 ethnic Germans emigrated to America from homes on the Russian steppes—flat, dry terrain that resembled the prairies of the Dakotas. Their ancestors had been lured to Russia by the promises of rulers Catherine the Great (reigned

In the 1870s ethnic Germans whose families had lived in Russia for 100 years began emigrating to the Great Plains of the United States and Canada. The so-called Volga Germans developed the region into the breadbasket of the continent, making the town of Eureka, Dakota Territory (shown here in 1887), a hub for wheat distribution.

1762–96) and Alexander I (1801–25), who wanted German farmers to cultivate the untilled steppes, and, later, according to her invitation, to "serve as models for agricultural occupations and handicrafts." Among the incentives were promises of religious liberty, exemption from military duty, cash grants, and self-government. There were 300 colonies of German settlers in southern Russia, scattered along the lower Volga River and in the Black Sea district, when in 1870 the czarist government began to revoke their original privileges.

The inhabitants of these colonies lived a life separate from their Russian neighbors and closely tied to their church, a pattern they duplicated in North America in independent communities of Lutheran, Catholic, or Mennonite persuasion. Most of those who chose the United States as their home (many Mennonites went to Canada because it granted them exemption from the draft), settled between the Missouri and Mississippi rivers to the east and the Rocky Mountains to the west. The isolation of Russian Germans in this area naturally slowed their assimilation into American society, but their success in farming the inhospitable land was key to the development of the Great Plains as the "granary of the world." By 1920, 420,000 of them lived in America, spread across most of the United States and in the western provinces of Canada. Russian Germans, who had introduced a variety of grain called red hard winter wheat from Turkey to the Volga River region, then grew the crop on their farms in the Dakotas, Nebraska, Kansas, and Colorado. In so doing, they helped make the United States self-sufficient in food production to this day.

Urban Tensions

Not everyone who arrived in the 1880s met with such opportunity. In the city as well as in the countryside, the average German immigrant found fewer acres and less work than had greeted his predecessors. Industrial-

The pickle-packing room of the H. J. Heinz factory in Pittsburgh, Pennsylvania, about 1900. Women were paid one penny per jar packed. The Heinz company, founded by a German immigrant, was notably beneficent to its workers.

ization was altering life in American cities much as it was in Germany. Artisans such as bakers, furniture workers, and toolmakers found their age-old skills of little value—factory work required the speedy completion of one small task, not a craftsman's painstaking care. A 12-year-old boy who had begun to learn the meticulous skills of cabinetmaking, for instance, might now stand for years at a machine repeatedly making one small item.

This trend led to high unemployment and to living conditions that were often miserable. In 1884, one German cigar maker in Chicago could find only occasional work; his family of eight lived in a three-room house that was "scantily and poorly furnished, no carpets, and the furniture being of the cheapest kind." His children were sick "at all times." Workers who found permanent employment could take little pride in their work and were often exploited. A conductor who put in a 16-hour day protested that "the company is grinding [me] and all the others down to the starvation point."

Nor did city officials make the workers' plight any easier. During the last decades of the 19th century, Chicago was the scene of repeated police abuse and election fraud. Meetings organized by workers were often disrupted by police, and police harassment and violence were used to get striking workers back on the job. The German newspapers of the day reported many cases in which politicians moved voting places overnight to prevent workers from voting in the morning, closed them before the workday ended, intimidated those who did arrive, and stuffed ballot boxes with illegal votes. The German-language newspaper *Verbote* responded indignantly to a blatant case of vote fraud in 1880: "We are fully justifed in saying that the holiest institution of the American people, the right to vote, has been desecrated and become a miserable farce and a lie."

These disillusioning events, coupled with poor living and working conditions, encouraged German immigrants to turn to labor unions as organizations that could best represent their interests. In 1886, almost one-third of the total union membership in Chicago was German, and of all the ethnic groups, Germans contributed the most members. In fact, more Germans joined labor unions in that city than did native-born Americans.

German involvement in the labor movement did not sit well with nativists, who, in the last decades of the 19th century, were again seeking support for anti-immigration laws. With the railroad strike of 1877 and the Haymarket Riot of May 4, 1886 (which broke out when someone at a workers' protest threw a bomb at policemen, who fired randomly in response), nativists claimed that German immigrants—with their predilection for socialism and radical labor activism—had imported the trouble. Though it was never determined who threw the bomb, eight men were tried in the wake of the Haymarket Riot; four were subsequently hanged, three of them German-born. This fact fueled the nativists' fire, as did the surge in German (and other) immigration in the 1880s.

Germans were highly active in labor causes in many big cities, but labor organizers got a bad name when an anarchist's bomb disrupted a rally at Haymarket Square in Chicago, Illinois, in 1886. Police fired on the crowd, and three Germans and an American were later hanged, though the bomb-thrower's identity was never proved.

United Germany: Inspiration and Threat

The unification of Germany by the Prussian prime minister Otto von Bismarck in 1871 focused American attention abroad long before World War I broke out in 1914. Some Germans in the United States were unenthusiastic: German-American Catholics in particular grew bitter at the oppressive measures the "Iron Chancellor" used to achieve his ends, and many emigrants now left the German empire in order to avoid being drafted into the Prussian army. But other German Americans overlooked Bismarck's failings, which they felt were exaggerated by the English-language press, and emphasized instead his leadership in the defeat of the French in the Franco-Prussian War of 1870–71 and the creation of a united Germany.

In fact, to an outspoken minority of German Americans, the event was an inspiration. If Germany could be united, they reasoned, why could not the diverse groups of Germans in America—never before united politically, but sharing a language, and to a large extent, a culture—act as a potent and unified bloc? A speaker in Cincinnati expressed this viewpoint by urging his compatriots to "make an end to all our petty quarrels. . . . Let us make our power felt, and let us use it wisely."

By the 1890s, this sentiment became more popular and was echoed in many of the 800 German-language publications across America, which shifted the focus of their news away from America and back to the fatherland. In part, this nationalism was in response to a sharp drop in German immigration at the end of the 19th century. This led to fears among some German Americans that without strong efforts to promote German culture their communities would assimilate completely, and the German language as well as German art, music, and literature would no longer have a presence in the United States. Promoting German culture did not mean abandoning the new homeland; indeed, many German Americans believed that the national interests of Germany and the United States were complementary, so that support for the one would ultimately benefit the other.

Native-born Americans grew increasingly wary of this German political and cultural activity in their midst. Nativist groups such as the Immigration Restriction League and the American Protective Association sought to limit immigration and supported measures—the prohibition of alcohol, woman suffrage (most suffragettes advocated prohibition), legislation requiring all students to speak English—that German Americans opposed.

German Americans responded by forming their own organizations, most notably the German-American National Alliance, founded in 1907 by an American-born engineer from Philadelphia named Charles J. Hexamer. Nativists, though, heard in the Alliance an echo of Germany's own Pan-German League, part of whose platform was "to oppose the united commercial power of our enemies, the Anglo-Saxons." Could Germany be trying to establish a power base in the Western Hemisphere, using German Americans as an advance guard?

Suspicions were fed by American fears of Germany's leader Kaiser Wilhelm, who had come to power in 1890 and whose militarism led many to believe he was bent on world domination. To a growing number of Americans, German-American unity seemed an expression of support for the Kaiser's imperialistic path, or at least a

When Chancellor Otto von Bismarck completed the unification of the German states in 1871, feeling for their homeland resurged among many German Americans. This in turn aroused new antiforeign sentiment in the United States.

sign of split loyalties. As early as 1894, in a speech entitled "What 'Americanism' Means," future president Theodore Roosevelt denounced immigrants who regarded themselves as "Irish-Americans" or "German-Americans." In his view, they were distinctly unpatriotic: "Some Americans need hyphens in their names because only part of them has come over. But when the whole man has come over, heart and thought and all, the hyphen drops of its own weight out of his name."

The term *hyphenate* became an increasingly popular insult to describe just about anybody who felt strongly about his ethnic identity. Ethnic tensions in America increased in August 1914 when fighting broke out in Europe. President Woodrow Wilson initially set the nation on a course of neutrality, urging that Americans be "impartial in thought as well as in action . . . neutral in fact as well as in name." But before the war was one month old, reports of German atrocities in Belgium (especially the burning of Louvain, with its ancient library) shocked many Americans and emboldened the American caricature of the goose-stepping, brutal Hun. *Life* magazine published a cartoon in late July 1915 that fueled this stereotype: a German officer with pointed helmet struts across the page; suspended from his bloody bayonet are an old man, a woman, and two small children. German submarines prowled the Atlantic, and by the time one sank the British passenger ship *Lusitania* in May 1915, killing 1,200 persons (including 124 American citizens), Wilson was hard put to recommend neutrality in thought or deed.

The vocal leadership of the German-American community inadvertently worsened tensions. The depredations of Belgium, they believed, had been exaggerated by Germany's enemies, especially Great Britain, in a deliberate attempt to draw the United States into the war—an attempt made all the easier by the two nations' common language and Wilson's noted allegiance to English culture. The publisher of the German-language

Omaha Tribüne, Val Peter, reflected this mentality in a 1915 address to the Nebraska branch of the German-American National Alliance:

> Both here and abroad, the enemy is the same! perfidious Albion [England]! Over there England has pressed the sword into the hands of almost all the peoples of Europe against Germany. In this country it has a servile press at its command, which uses every foul means to slander everything German and to poison the public mind.

But by dismissing every reported atrocity as anti-German propaganda and portraying the nation's leadership (especially President Wilson) as unsuspecting dupes of the British, prominent German Americans came across to the American public as callous, uncaring, and undiscriminating in their support of Germany. For example, although most German-American newspapers and organizations expressed dismay over the lives that had been lost when the *Lusitania* was torpedoed, they also made excuses for the German action: United States citizens had been warned by the German embassy about traveling on British ships; Germany was forced into submarine warfare by the British blockade of Germany; Congress should have ensured a policy of strict neutrality by forbidding the sale of American weapons to the British. These excuses rang hollow to many Americans who were distraught over the tragic loss of life.

President Wilson vigorously repaid the attacks on him in the German-American press with a number of speeches made in the fall of 1915. In his State of the Union address to Congress that year, Wilson condemned "citizens of the United States, . . . who have poured the poison of disloyalty into the very arteries of our national life; who have sought to bring the authority and good name of our Government into contempt." With language that was more characteristic of the fiery Roosevelt, Wilson went on to insist that all such traitors "must be crushed out," and that "the hand of our power should close over them at once." Wilson's speeches, implicitly equating support of Germany with treasonous anti-Americanism, marked the beginning of the end of American neutrality.

The United States entered World War I on April 6, 1917, with this declaration by President Wilson: "The world must be made safe for democracy . . . the right is more precious than peace." He had been driven to declare war, he told Congress, by Germany's continuation of submarine warfare. But there was another major factor in Wilson's decision. A telegram, written by German foreign minister Arthur Zimmermann and sent to Mexico, had been intercepted by the British navy. In the telegram Germany offered to help Mexico regain Texas, Arizona, and New Mexico, a plan evidently designed to keep U.S. troops out of Germany's backyard by keeping them busy at home. The telegram convinced both Wilson and the American public of Germany's hostile intentions toward the United States. Unfortunately, like many of Germany's actions during World War I, it sparked hatred of all things German. As American soldiers—many of German descent—arrived on the battlefields of Europe, anti-German hysteria welled up in cities, towns, and rural outposts across America.

Anti-Germanism Grows Violent

On the night of April 4, 1918, a year after the United States had declared war against Germany, a group of Maryville, Illinois, coal miners apprehended Robert Paul Prager, a co-worker whom they suspected of being a German spy. They marched him from his home in Collinsville, forced him to kiss the American flag and to sing patriotic songs in front of a gathering crowd, and questioned him about his activities as a German spy. Prager insisted on his innocence and on his loyalty to the United States. But the mob was not appeased, and they hanged him from a tree on the outskirts of town.

Despite much hostility in both popular and official circles to unrestricted immigration, Germans continued to cross the Atlantic in droves between 1865 and 1914. A German immigrant artist depicts the main reason: In America, By Industry We Thrive.

Prager's death was the culmination of a year of harassment of German Americans. Theodore Ladenburger, a German Jew living in New York, wrote that "from the moment that the United States had declared war on Germany," he was made to feel like "a traitor to [his] adopted country." Moreover, he continued:

> . . . in view of my record as a citizen I did expect from my neighbors and fellow citizens a fair estimate and appreciation of my honesty and trustworthiness. It had all vanished. Outstanding was the only fact, of which I was never ashamed—nor did I ever make a secret of it—that I had been born in Germany.

German Americans were intimidated into buying Liberty Bonds (sold by the U.S. Treasury to finance the war), imprisoned for making "disloyal" remarks, and forced to participate in flag-kissing ceremonies like the

Anti-German feeling heated up markedly after America's entry into World War I in 1917. Robert Prager, a German-born coal miner in Illinois, was accused by a mob of spying for the kaiser and was lynched.

one that preceded Prager's lynching. Citizens from Florida to California were publicly flogged or tarred and feathered. Homes and schools were vandalized. Mennonites, who firmly opposed all wars, were especially persecuted; in 1917–18, more than 1,500 Mennonites fled the United States to settle in Canada.

Hysteria also threatened German cultural institutions. Attacks on German music included the banning of Beethoven in Pittsburgh and the arrest of Dr. Karl Muck, the German-born conductor of the Boston Symphony, on charges that he was a threat to the safety of the country. The same motive lay behind the removal or vandalism of statues of poets Johann Goethe and Friedrich Schiller and other German cultural giants. German-language classes were dropped from school curricula and German textbooks banned. Under a 1917 law, German-language newspapers had to supply English-language translations that were reviewed for approval by local postmasters. If the material was found to be unacceptable, mailing privileges were withdrawn.

Perhaps the most ridiculous example of the rush to "de-Germanize" America was the removal, in 1917, of the figure of the goddess Germania from the Germania Life Insurance Building in St. Paul, Minnesota. The building was renamed the Guardian Building. Likewise, streets, parks, schools, and even towns were rechristened: Germantown, Nebraska, for example, became Garland, and Berlin, Iowa, was renamed Lincoln. Restaurants served "liberty steak" in place of hamburgers and "liberty cabbage" for sauerkraut. In Massachusetts, a physician even renamed German measles "liberty measles."

What were some of the other effects of such widespread anti-German hysteria? The German-American National Alliance faltered in April 1918, the month of Robert Prager's death, and membership in German cultural and political organizations plummeted. Many German Americans stopped speaking German, even in the privacy of their homes. German aliens rushed to become American citizens, and hundreds of citizens of

German descent changed their names. George Washington Ochs of Philadelphia petitioned to change his last name to Oakes, despite the patriotism clearly embodied in his first two names.

Exceptions to this wave of hasty assimilation included tight-knit groups of churchgoing Germans, who reacted by clinging more firmly to their beliefs and customs and by isolating themselves further from their neighbors. After the armistice of November 11, 1918, church groups risked American hostility by doing relief work in Germany, where starvation threatened thousands of people. This work, which consisted mainly of raising money for food and clothing to be sent to Germany, stimulated a brief revival of ethnic consciousness. United by their concern for friends and relatives abroad, German Americans contributed heavily to relief programs.

But organizations such as the Steuben Society, founded in New York in 1919 and guided by aims of political unity similar to those pursued by prewar groups, never became really popular again. Even before the war broke out, German Americans had been assimilating apace, learning English and seeking careers in the larger American society. Indeed, by the 20th century, sizable communities where only German was spoken were largely a thing of the past. But in the opinion of at least one historian, World War I did not simply hasten this assimilation, it virtually banished ethnic consciousness among German Americans so that the postwar generation suffered from a kind of "cultural amnesia": parents who were immigrants or first-generation Americans had—out of fear and humiliation—so denied their roots that their children grew up with no sense of their own German heritage.

The hysteria ignited by the war led to the removal of the statue of the mythic goddess Germania from the Old Germania Life Insurance Building in St. Paul, Minnesota; the building was then renamed. In this era, some German Americans changed their own names and disavowed their cultural heritage.

Up and Down with the Press

That heritage was most palpably conveyed by German Americans who had founded, edited, and contributed to periodicals printed in the German language. Publishers generally had a high sense of responsibility toward their readers; all of them tried to better the lot of their countrymen. Their job was twofold. They worked to preserve German language and culture as long as possible; they also tried to introduce their readers to American social and political life.

Even in colonial times, this mission was met: Between 1732 and 1800 there were 38 German-language newspapers published in the United States. The heyday of the German-American press, however, came in the years between 1848 and 1860, when there were 266 German newspapers. This amazing growth is explained in part by the huge number of new immigrants, but more significant was the arrival of the forty-eighters.

Many of these political refugees had edited or written for radical newspapers in Germany; most regarded the press as a force for social change. More than half of their ranks became involved in some aspect of journalism in the United States. Their high standards and their emphasis on politics sometimes shook up the German-American publishers who had been in the business for years. In Cincinnati, for example, there was sub-

PUBLIC LEDGER

PHILADELPHIA, SUNDAY MORNING, MARCH 2, 1913.

WHAT OUR GERMANIC POPULATION IS DOING FOR AMERICA

The 15,000,000 German-Americans Lead All Other Nationalities in 29 States, and in Many Industries They Are at the Top—Race Was Here Before the Pilgrims

CHARLES J. HEXAMER
President of the National German-American Alliance.

CHARLES M. SCHWAB
President of the Bethlehem Steel Company.

HENRY C. FRICK
A Leader in the Coal and Transportation Industries.

REAR ADMIRAL HUGO OSTERHAUS, U. S. N.

TO THE GERMANS WE OWE:

The first Bible printed on this continent.
The first protest against slavery.
Our first steel mill, our first paper mill and our first iron foundry.
Our first chemical and leather factories.
That famous purchase of Manhattan Island from the Indians for $24.

OUR GERMAN POPULATION

In 29 of the 48 States leads all other foreign nationalities.
Forms 22 per cent. of the total white population of the United States.

Serious German-American journalism dates to the early 1700s, but it got its biggest boost from the great number of "forty-eighters" who entered the trade. In the tense World War I years, one Philadelphia publisher let it be known that Germans had helped build the American nation.

stantial rivalry between the incoming "Greens" and the old guard publishers, or "Grays," who were quite comfortable with the idea of the foreign-language newspaper as a meek forum of social announcements and sentimental stories and poems about the old country. Elsewhere, however, the two factions coexisted peaceably or even worked together on papers that became powerful in the community. In St. Louis, where there were seven German dailies in 1860, forty-eighters joined the staffs of *Die Waage* and *Anzeiger des Westens*, and the latter was transformed into an antislavery journal by three immigrants.

This journalistic tradition spawned many advances. Thomas Nast, the son of a forty-eighter, is known as the father of the political cartoon and was the first person to depict a donkey and elephant as mascots of the Democratic and Republican parties. Ottmar Mergenthaler invented the Linotype, an automatic typesetting machine that had its first successful run on July 3, 1886, in the composing room of the *New York Tribune*.

The number of German publications reached its peak in 1894 at 800 and began a rapid decline hinging on the political tension in Europe. Between 1910 and 1920, the number of German-language publications in America dropped from 554 to 234. Subscribers fell away, especially with President Wilson's declaration of war in 1917, and many were not won back even at war's end.

Hiding Their Ancestry

German reading matter was not the only casualty of the war at home; ethnic pride suffered, too, as shown by a strange twist in the 1920 U.S. census. Although in the preceding decade 174,227 newcomers arrived from Germany (most of them in 1910–14, before the outbreak of the war) and return migration was low, the statistics show a 25.3 percent *decline* from the 1910 census in the number of German-born Americans. According to historian La Vern J. Rippley, the discrepancy can be

A bottling room at the Schlitz Brewery in Milwaukee, Wisconsin. The Prohibition years (1919–33) were particularly (and intentionally) hard on German Americans, who controlled most U.S. breweries.

explained by the reluctance of German Americans to reveal their birthplace to 1920 census takers. Rippley concludes that "the German-born as well as the German stock in the United States moved underground."

The 1920s brought another set of challenges to the immigrant population. Legal persecution of Germans died down, and, in 1923, the U.S. Supreme Court declared legislation banning the teaching of German in schools unconstitutional. But anti-German sentiment created a more lasting legacy with the passage of the Eighteenth Amendment, ratified on July 1, 1919, which prohibited the manufacture and sale of alcoholic drinks. Many backers of the amendment were genuinely concerned about the host of social and public health problems caused by alcoholism. But others were motivated by a desire to restrict an activity that was viewed by Germans and non-Germans alike as a central part of German-American social life and to curtail the economic success of the German Americans who owned most of the nation's breweries.

Retaliation came safely in one place—the voting booth. It appears that in 1920, German Americans, ethnically minded or not, gained some measure of revenge for Wilson's wartime policies by casting their votes not so much *for* presidential candidate Warren G. Harding as *against* Wilson's fellow Democrat James Cox. Harding's candidacy was publicly and strongly backed by the *Deutsch-Amerikanische Burgerbund*, or the German-American Citizen's League, which openly resolved to "sweep from office all miscreants . . . who hounded and persecuted Americans of German descent, . . . who [are] contemptuous of any hyphen except the one which binds them to Great Britain, unmindful of the supreme sacrifice of Americans of German blood in the late war."

Established in Chicago in January 1921, the radical *Burgerbund* was a rarity in the postwar period. Some of its diehards thought that Harding owed his victory to the German-American vote, and five of them visited the vacationing president-elect in Florida to demand a seat in his cabinet. The demand went unmet.

By 1924, the *Burgerbund* had retreated, and leadership of the community fell to the more moderate Steuben Society. Founded in 1919, the society aimed to shift blame for the war from Germany onto Russia and France. In this effort it was aided by a group of revisionist writers and historians who held that Germany was not solely responsible for the bloodshed. But the Steuben Society's more immediate goal was to recast the image of the German American in the eyes of the general public. German Americans, the society's members insisted, were neither "mongrels with a divided allegiance" nor "hyphenates." In keeping with this goal, they named their organization after Baron Friedrich von Steuben, a hero of the War of Independence. By the 1924 election the so-called revenge vote had run its course, with German Americans once again casting their ballots diversely.

The shambles of the postwar economy in Germany caused hyperinflation in 1922 and 1923. This Berlin housewife uses a pile of worthless banknotes to light the morning fire.

After the War's Disgrace

Postwar Germany was a shambles: 1,800,000 people had died during the war and more than twice that number were wounded. Its economy was also in ruins—from July to November 1923, the value of the German mark plummeted from 160,000 marks to the dollar to 4.2 billion marks to the dollar. Life again looked more secure across the Atlantic, and about 430,000 German immigrants came to the United States between 1919 and 1933. The majority were fleeing the hopeless economic situation, but some left for political reasons—Germany's postwar constitution displeased leftists and rightists alike.

Among the émigrés in these years were increasing numbers of German Jews, fleeing the resurgence of anti-Semitism in Germany. Jews had always been discriminated against in Germany, but by the early 20th century German anti-Semitism had become fairly muted. German Jews were excluded from most government-related careers, for example, but could still make a good living in the prestigious independent professions of medicine, law, journalism, and the arts. Most German Jews spoke German rather than Hebrew or Yiddish, and many considered themselves more German than Jewish.

But as the economic situation in Germany deteriorated, German Jews found themselves increasingly being blamed for all that had gone wrong during the war and afterwards. Much of this scapegoating was the work of Adolf Hitler's National Socialist German Workers' Party (NSDAP)—the Nazi party. The Nazis wanted, in their words, to "purify" Germany of Jews, gypsies, Slavs, and other "non-Aryan" races, as well as of homosexuals and political liberals, making it the private sanctum of fair-haired "Aryan" Germans. Nazi sympathizers tended to be young, lower-middle-class men who counted themselves among the "lost generation"—people whose lives and opportunities had been shattered by the war. Not surprisingly, some supporters and members of the Nazi party came to the United States in search of better opportunities, and in 1924, four recent newcomers founded the Teutonia Association in Detroit, where they had gone to seek work. During the next two years, the organization attracted others who had already been active in Hitler's circle in Germany. By 1932, the group had branches in five American cities and a membership of more than 500.

Many of that number expected to return to Germany once Hitler came to power, and the association, at least initially, did not regard itself as a vehicle for spreading National Socialism in the United States. In 1936, however, another organization was formed with that very aim. It was called the German-American Bund, known generally as the *Bund*, and its members were known as Bundists.

Leaders of American Nazi organizations shared Hitler's distorted view of the United States and of the 8 million Americans of German stock who lived there. They thought it their duty to "rescue" their Aryan brothers from the insidious influence of American culture, Jews, and communists. They expected, ignoring the extent of intermarriage and the variety of American political and racial opinion, that German Americans would heed their cry en masse.

In actuality, Americans of German descent seemed no more influenced by Nazi propaganda than anyone else. In the 1930s, one pollster found that 70 percent of the German Americans he interviewed were "totally indifferent" to international Nazism and that 20 percent were "definitely anti-Nazi." Bund membership never exceeded 25,000, and most of that number was concentrated in the industrial cities of the Northeast, where newcomers tended to congregate. The impression that the Bund was more powerful than it actually was from 1936 to 1939 stemmed from wide coverage on radio and in the newspapers.

The Bund's racist assertions, calling for an America ruled only by white Christians, eventually brought it under investigation by the U.S. House of Representatives' Committee on Un-American Activities. In late 1939 Bund leader Fritz Kuhn was convicted of stealing organization funds. When the United States entered World War II in 1941, Kuhn was in prison and the Bund was waning rapidly.

The Bund's downfall is easily explained: Few German Americans responded to its call for collective racial action based on the notion of Aryan supremacy. In Milwaukee, for example, the Bund received so much negative publicity in the German-language *Journal* that it was soon forced to hold its meetings outside the city. The chairman of the New York branch of the Steuben Society denounced the Bundists as "unfortunately of our blood, but of no credit to us."

After Hitler's rise to power in 1933, religion once again became a reason to emigrate. Jewish shops and merchants in Germany were the object of rampaging attacks on Kristallnacht *in 1938, in which 191 synagogues, 814 stores, and 171 Jewish homes were destroyed. Thousands of non-Jews also fled Germany and Austria.*

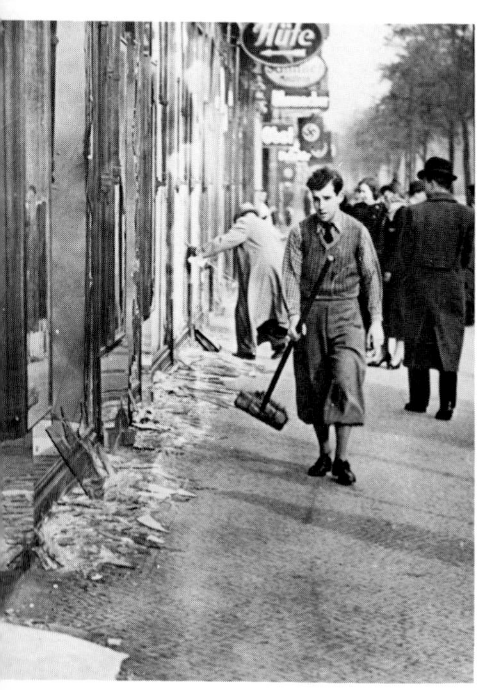

When Hitler became chancellor of Germany in January 1933, the event provoked some short-lived hostility in New York—Jews boycotted German-owned stores and German-made goods, and Christian German Americans responded by boycotting Jewish shops and services. When the Bund got involved in the boycott, however, most Christian German Americans shied away. But by the end of the decade, Nazi atrocities had drawn the entire world's attention. American opinion began to shift noticeably in March 1938 when Hitler invaded and annexed neighboring Austria. Then, 8 months later, Nazis across Germany burned more than 500 synagogues and looted or destroyed Jewish stores; thousands of Jews were beaten, shot, and dragged off to concentration camps.

Expressions of anger issued from all over the United States. President Roosevelt recalled the U.S. ambassador to Germany and protested to the Nazi government. (Less nobly, the United States—along with many European nations—closed its borders to all but a handful of Jewish refugees.) The Steuben Society issued its first unqualified public denouncement of Nazi anti-Semitism. On November 15, the New York *Staats-Zeitung,* the most influential German-language newspaper of its day, spoke out against the "dark powers" that would "turn loose the lowest and most degraded instincts against defenseless people."

When war broke out in Europe in September 1939, many members of the German-American community—as they had before U.S. entry into the previous war—called for an isolationist policy. So, unfortunately, did the pro-Nazi Bundists. This coincidence of opinion (one side anti-Semitic, the other antiwar) did not reflect well on the German-American community as a whole, and the non-Bundists feared a replay of the anti-Germanism that swept America during World War I.

No matter what reasons the isolationists had, America's entrance into the war seemed inevitable as Hitler's forces invaded more of Europe. By January 1941, two-thirds of all Americans favored supporting Great Britain against Germany and Italy. Partly in response to this growing public sentiment, and to convince Americans of their loyalty, some German-American societies agreed. Robert F. Wagner, later the mayor of New York and son of the German-born New York senator of the same name, headed a group called the Loyal Americans of German Descent. Formed in July 1941, it pledged to "rally all our fellow-citizens of German ancestry to the all-out defense of America and of democracy."

With the Japanese attack on Pearl Harbor on December 7, 1941, the United States entered the war. Organizations that had urged isolationism all along were quick to declare their loyalty to the American cause. The *Steuben News*, for example, devoted its entire January 1942 issue to expressions of support for the war effort. As during World War I, some German Americans exercised their right to oppose U.S. involvement, but when involvement came, they generally supported the cause. With few exceptions, nothing close to the widespread anti-German hysteria of the World War I years occurred during World War II.

The reasons were various. This war had been started not by the German empire, but by one radical political party led by an apparent madman. And by the 1940s, after 20 years of low German immigration, German Americans for the most part spoke English and participated in mainstream politics and society; many had Anglicized their names to prevent a recurrence of the random persecution. World War II was a supreme national cause, one in which German Americans loyally took part.

Fritz Kuhn, leader of the German American Bund, addresses a rally of pro-Nazi Americans at Madison Square Garden in New York City, 1939. Far more numerous than Nazi sympathizers were the Loyal Americans of German Descent, a group founded by a German immigrant's son, Robert F. Wagner, who was later mayor of New York.

Here, a group of German-American atomic researchers—refugees of World War II—pose at the White Sands Proving Ground in New Mexico.

THE GERMAN-AMERICAN CONTRIBUTION

I wish to remain in the U.S.A. and become an American citizen. After almost twelve years of enforced wandering, one has the desire to have a home and a base to stand on; my children have already become completely American in mind and behavior and I wish to give them the legal rights an American citizen enjoys. For myself I desire the feeling of security—to be at home some place in the world.

—anonymous German actor
who came to America in 1941

Given the large numbers of Germans who have immigrated into the United States since colonial times, it is hardly surprising that individual German Americans have made notable contributions in every field of endeavor. The annals of American history are laden with names of German extraction: paper manufacturer Frederick Weyerhaeuser, leaders of the United Automobile Workers union and the Congress of Industrial Organizations Walter and Victor Reuther, condiments magnate H. J. Heinz, President Dwight D. Eisenhower, and baseball manager Casey Stengel, to name just a few.

German Americans altered the landscape in the New World not only as individuals; the group as a whole brought customs now considered part of the American way. German settlers in the middle Atlantic states in the

18th century built the first log cabins in this wilderness, replicating a custom from the German forests. Their method of fitting the logs with V-notches and of filling cracks with cement became a standard defense against snow in Wisconsin or dust in Texas, two states where some of the original structures may still be seen. And the most colorful of Christian holidays, Christmas, was not elaborately observed in the United States until the late 19th century, when the German customs of raising the *Tannenbaum* (Christmas tree) and eulogizing Kris Kringle (Santa Claus) caught on. Picnic food is chiefly German in origin—frankfurters, hamburgers, sauerkraut, and potato salad.

Altogether, the accomplishments of individual German immigrants form an important part of the history of the United States—and of the world.

German immigrants brought the Christmas tree to the New World, but their custom, dating from the 1600s, became common in North America only in the late 1800s. Around the same time, a German-born cartoonist, Thomas Nast, sketched what is now the popular image of St. Nick.

The Power of the Pen

One immigrant remembered for championing the cause of free speech was John Peter Zenger, who came to New York at age 13 in 1710 from the Palatinate. Like many

John Peter Zenger went on trial in 1735 for publishing uncomplimentary opinions about the British colonial governor of New York. Zenger's lawyer, Andrew Hamilton (with arm extended), successfully defended him on the principle that criticism of officials, if true, is not illegal.

an immigrant child of the 1709 exodus, Zenger was advertised as an orphan and apprenticed, in his case to printer William Bradford, whose lofty post in the colony was granted by King George I of England. In 1725, Bradford published New York's first newspaper, the *New York Gazette,* and under his tutelage Zenger rose from apprentice to paid employee to partner. In 1733, the partnership dissolved and Zenger established the colony's first independent newspaper, the *New-York Weekly Journal.* In one of the journal's first issues, Zenger called Bradford's *New York Gazette* "a paper known to be under the direction of the government, in which the Printer of it is not suffered to insert anything but what his superiors approve of."

To make the point, Zenger's paper published absolutely nothing that Governor William Cosby could approve of. Each issue was filled with attacks on Cosby and his policies, often in the form of phony letters to the editor or bogus advertisements for lost pets that were actually clever ways of calling the governor a monkey and his associates spaniels.

Two months of this kind of publicity were enough to convince Cosby that he had to take action. On August 4, 1735, he managed to bring Zenger to trial on charges of libel. Andrew Hamilton, Zenger's lawyer, argued that public criticism of government officials, as long as it was

Scion of a Baltimore family of tobacco merchants, H. L. Mencken opted instead for a career as reporter, critic, and editor. His masterpiece, The American Language, *grew out of his studies of native and immigrant speech across the country.*

true, was a safeguard of American liberties. His argument was so persuasive that the jury returned a verdict of not guilty after only a few minutes of deliberation, and Zenger was free to print a full account of his trial in the *Journal.* The trial set a precedent that has given the United States a press the least shackled by government of any in the world.

Zenger's appreciation for the power of the press was shared by a later German-American writer, perhaps this century's most renowned and provocative journalist, Henry Louis Mencken. In 1936, Mencken returned to his childhood home in Baltimore. In his father's files he discovered the bill for a Christmas present he had received in 1887: a printing press and a set of type.

"That press," Mencken recalled in *Happy Days,* the first volume of his memoirs, "determined the whole course of my future life. If it had been a stethoscope or a copy of Dr. Ayers' Almanac I might have gone in for medicine; if it had been a Greek New Testament or a set of baptismal grappling-irons I might have pursued divinity. As it was, I got the smell of printer's ink up my nose at the tender age of seven, and it has been swirling through my sinuses ever since."

Mencken's career in journalism broke with family tradition. His grandfather Burkhardt Ludwig Mencken had arrived in Baltimore from Germany in 1848. He began as a cigar dealer's apprentice; less than a decade later he owned a wholesale tobacco firm. Henry's father, August, was the proud owner of Aug. Mencken & Co., a cigar manufacturing company in Baltimore. When Henry graduated from high school, everyone (except the boy) assumed he would become the third generation of Menckens in the tobacco industry.

But when Mencken landed his first job with the Baltimore *Morning Herald* in 1899, he joined a long line of German Americans who made their living from the printed word. With his biting wit and his willingness to turn it on any subject or personage, Mencken's daring, intelligent, and honest prose set a standard for American journalists. He maintained a lifelong association with Baltimore newspapers, served as editor of various magazines, and in 1924 cofounded another, *The American Mercury*. He pursued his wide range of interests by writing books on democracy, philosophy, and religion, as well as a book of poetry and many volumes of memoirs and diaries.

Mencken's greatest work was *The American Language*, begun in 1918 and later expanded and revised. In it he described with great scholarship and verve the makeup of the national argot, the alterations in pronunciation over the decades, and the thousands of words added to the American vocabulary by the dozens of immigrant groups he listened to around the country. The work has become outdated, but it has never been surpassed as a study of a vibrant culture and language.

A 1733 issue of Zenger's paper, the New-York Weekly Journal. *The author of the lead editorial, writing on the topic "Liberty of the Press," draws the distinction between an absolute monarchy and a limited monarchy, which England was considered to be.*

Numb. II.

THE

New-York Weekly JOURNAL.

Containing the freſheſt Advices, Foreign, and Domeſtick.

MUNDAY November 12, 1733.

Mr. *Zenger.*

INcert the following in your next, and you'll oblige your Friend,

CATO.

Mira temporum felicitas ubi ſentiri quæ velis, & quæ ſentias dicere licit.

Tacit.

THE Liberty of the Preſs is a Subject of the greateſt Importance, and in which every Individual is as much concern'd as he is in any other Part of Liberty: Therefore it will not be improper to communicate to the Publick the Sentiments of a late excellent Writer upon this Point. ſuch is the Elegance and Perſpicuity of his Writings, ſuch the inimitable Force of his Reaſoning, that it will be difficult to ſay any Thing new that he has not ſaid, or not to ſay that much worſe which he has ſaid.

There are two Sorts of Monarchies, an abſolute and a limited one. In the firſt, the Liberty of the Preſs can never be maintained, it is inconſiſtent with it; for what abſolute Monarch would ſuffer any Subject to animadvert on his Actions, when it is in his Power to declare the Crime, and to nominate the Puniſhment? This would make it very dangerous to exerciſe ſuch a Liberty Beſides the Object againſt which thoſe Pens muſt be directed, is

their Sovereign, the ſole ſupream Ma-
giſtrate; for there being no Law in
thoſe Monarchies, but the Will of the
Prince, it makes it neceſſary for his
Miniſters to conſult his Pleaſure, before any Thing can be undertaken:
He is therefore properly chargeable
with the Grievances of his Subjects,
and what the Miniſter there acts being
in Obedience to the Prince, he ough
not to incur the Hatred of the People
for it would be hard to impute that t
him for a Crime, which is the Fruit c
his Allegiance, and for refuſing which
he might incur the Penalties of Trea
ſon. Beſides, in an abſolute Monar
chy, the Will of the Prince being th
Law, a Liberty of the Preſs to complai
of Grievances would be complainin
againſt the Law, and the Conſtitution
to which they have ſubmitted, or hav
been obliged to ſubmit; and therefore
in one Senſe, may be ſaid to deſerv
Puniſhment, So that under an abſo
lute Monarchy, I ſay, ſuch a Libert
is inconſiſtent with the Conſtitution
having no proper Subject in Politic
on which it might be exercis'd, and
exercis'd would incur a certain Penalty

But in a limited Monarchy, as *Eng
land* is, our Laws are known, fixed
and eſtabliſhed. They are the ſtreigh
Rule and ſure Guide to direct the King
the Miniſters, and other his Subjects
And therefore an Offence againſt th
Laws is ſuch an Offence againſt th
Conſtitution as ought to receive a pr
per adequate Puniſhment; the ſevera
Conſti

Planting the Seeds of Progress

German Americans did not only excel in letters. In many instances German-born citizens laid the foundations for scientific disciplines in the United States. American pediatricians, for example, point to forty-eighter Abraham Jacobi as the father of their profession. In the case of forestry and wilderness conservation, the science was unknown in America before the arrival of Bernhard Eduard Fernow in 1876. Anthropology was elevated from an amateur's hobby to a scholarly discipline in great part by the 40-year career of Franz Boas, a German who emigrated in 1888. Among his students at Columbia University were Ruth Benedict and Margaret Mead.

First Among Many: Carl Schurz

The career of one man comes closest, perhaps, to illuminating how a German upbringing matched so well the needs of a growing America. Carl Schurz first came to prominence in this country in the 1850s for expressing his strong antislavery views; he was firmly committed to securing justice for black Americans. Initially inspired by Lucretia Mott, the founder of the Philadelphia Female Anti-Slavery Society, Schurz took an active part in the abolitionist movement in 1856. At first he addressed crowds of midwestern German Americans in their (and his) native language. Three years later, he achieved national renown with "True Americanism," a speech he delivered before a huge audience in Boston's Faneuil Hall. He once declared, "I think it can be said without exaggeration that there has never been in the history of this Republic a political movement [the abolition of slavery] in which the purely moral motive was so strong—indeed, so dominant and decisive."

Though the slavery question propelled Schurz into American politics, his involvement with the causes of justice and freedom predated his emigration. As an 18-year-old student at the University of Bonn, he befriended a liberal professor named Gottfried Kinkel. Kinkel convinced the young Schurz of the necessity of revolution; after 50 years of autocratic rule, revolution seemed to him the only way to bring about a "united and more democratic government" in Germany. Schurz joined the effort, helping edit and publish Kinkel's newspaper, the *Bonner Zeitung,* and making his first public appearances in support of a political cause.

When the 1848 revolution came, however, it was quickly squashed. Kinkel was sentenced to life imprisonment, and Schurz was forced to flee to Switzerland. But, in response to an appeal from Kinkel's wife, Johanna, the 21-year-old Schurz returned to Germany and rescued his former professor from Spandau prison.

As an exile in England, Schurz met Margarethe Meyer, who was visiting London from Hamburg. They married in July 1852 and sailed for New York a month later. "The fatherland was closed to me," wrote Schurz. "England was to me a foreign country, and would always remain so. Where then? 'To America,' I said to myself." The newlyweds soon joined relatives in Watertown, Wisconsin. Margarethe opened the state's first kindergarten, and Carl set about teaching himself English and studying law. And, at about the same time that an Illinois representative named Abraham Lincoln became a member, Carl Schurz joined the newly formed Republican party.

Schurz campaigned vigorously for Lincoln in both the 1860 and 1864 presidential elections. "It is said that I made Lincoln president," he wrote to a friend in Germany. "This is certainly not true; but the fact that people say it indicates that I did contribute something toward raising the wind which bore Lincoln into the presidential chair and thus shook the slave-system to its very foundation." Lincoln appointed Schurz ambassador to Spain, a post he left in 1862 to counsel the president on how best to avoid foreign intervention in the Civil War. As it turned out, he offered both advice and military service, remaining in America as a brigadier general of volunteer Union troops.

Forty-eighter Carl Schurz was utterly dedicated to the causes of political reform, social improvements, and conservation. He reminded his fellow German Americans that "we as Germans are not called upon here to form a separate nationality but rather to contribute to the American nationality the strongest there is in us."

Lincoln's assassination in 1865 marked a milestone in Carl Schurz's career. Dissatisfied with Lincoln's successor, Andrew Johnson, Schurz left Washington and, like many of his fellow forty-eighters, turned to a career in journalism. The family moved to St. Louis, where Schurz assumed the editorship of *Die Westliche Post,* a German-language daily.

Schurz soon reentered politics. In 1869, he became the first German-born citizen to win election to the Senate. A senator from Missouri until 1875, he solidified his reputation as a highly principled defender of freedom. He fought United States expansion in the Caribbean, corruption in government, and unfair treatment of American Indians. As secretary of the interior in President Rutherford B. Hayes's cabinet, Schurz continued to champion those causes that had engaged him as a senator. He completely reorganized the Bureau of Indian Affairs, setting up much-needed educational programs for young Indians, and he instituted a policy to conserve forests and lands.

Schurz was at various times a journalist, lawyer, major general, ambassador, senator, and cabinet secretary. He also advised virtually every president from Abraham Lincoln to Theodore Roosevelt. Here he plays the piano for President Rutherford B. Hayes (seated at table) and family in the White House.

Building bridges was the forte of the Roebling family. John Roebling, immigrant farmer turned engineer, built the Niagara Bridge in the 1840s. The first suspension bridge to accommodate trains, it linked railroads in Ontario and New York.

Schurz's many friends and supporters included Mark Twain. When Schurz died on May 14, 1906, in New York City, Twain wrote a tribute to him in which he compared Schurz to a boyhood friend of his, Ben Thornburgh, who had been particularly adept at finding the best route through difficult waters. "More than once," Twain wrote about Ben, "I waited for him to find the way, then dropped into his steamer's wake and ran over the wrecks of his buoys on half steam until the leadsman's welcome cry of 'mark twain' informed me that I was over the bar all right, and could draw a full breath again."

Twain continued: "I had this same confidence in Carl Schurz as a political channel-finder. I had the highest opinion of his inborn qualifications for the office: his blemishless honor, his unassailable patriotism, his high intelligence, his penetration; I also had the highest opinion of his acquired qualifications as a channel finder. . . . I have not always sailed with him politically, but whenever I have doubted my own competency to choose the right course, I have . . . followed him through without doubt or hesitancy."

The Bridge

In 1831, with the urging of a friend, John Augustus Roebling left an unsatisfying job as a government surveyor

After illness permanently confined him to his house, Washington Roebling directed the fulfillment of his father's plans for the Brooklyn Bridge from his window. His wife Emily relayed his orders to the work site.

in Prussia and emigrated to the United States, settling with a colony of Saxons on land north of Pittsburgh. There he married Johanna Herting and they had a son—the first of nine children—whom they named Washington Augustus.

But pioneer farming did not suit Roebling. The many applications he filed with the U.S. Patent Office in these years suggest he was more interested in redesigning farm machinery than in operating it. So in 1837, he returned to his former career, taking a job as engineer of the state of Pennsylvania.

The Allegheny Mountains cut through the heart of Pennsylvania, presenting a formidable transportation problem. Boats traveling on the interior waterways of the day had to be transferred onto railroad cars, which were then hauled over mountain passes to the next watershed.

Roebling was overseeing one such operation when he witnessed an accident: the massive hemp rope drawing the railroad car snapped and the car hurtled back down the incline, killing two workers. What better way, he thought, to avert further mishaps than to manufacture a far stronger rope out of wire? He soon developed his own method of stranding and weaving wire cable, an innovation that both established his reputation and allowed him to embark on a career as a builder of suspension bridges, each more ambitious and striking than the last.

The suspension bridge lives up to its name. It is a roadway suspended from two or more heavy wire cables, which, in turn, pass over two towers that rise from a firm foundation beneath the water. Roebling's first bridge, built over Pittsburgh's Monongahela River in 1845, was also the first suspension bridge to be scientifically designed and constructed. His next major project was prompted by the rapid growth of the railroad in North America. Working through four brutal Canadian winters and a cholera epidemic, Roebling built the Niagara Bridge, the first suspension bridge to accommodate trains. It connected the Great Western Railway of Canada with the Rochester-Niagara lines of the New York Central Railroad.

Despite continuing interruptions—the 1857 depression and the Civil War—Roebling completed the Cincinnati Bridge on December 1, 1866. With a span of 1,051 feet, it was the longest bridge in the world, but Roebling's most celebrated suspension bridge, the Brooklyn Bridge, was still to come.

In 1854, Brooklyn, New York, was the fastest growing city in the country. Boats ferried passengers across the East River to Manhattan, but the need for a bridge between the two boroughs was increasingly apparent, and in 1869, Roebling began construction. In July, while he was making some preliminary calculations, his foot was crushed between two logs; although a doctor amputated all the toes of his right foot, tetanus set in and Roebling died within three weeks.

The bridge was finished by Washington Roebling, who, at great personal sacrifice, realized the design his father had seen only in blueprints. In 1872, after a 12-hour stint below water, the younger Roebling contracted caisson disease. Named after the watertight chamber that divers used to lay bridge foundations, caisson disease was common among workers who were raised too rapidly from great underwater depths. Roebling's case was so debilitating that he was forced to oversee the final years of construction from the window of his Brooklyn apartment, while his wife Emily personally issued his directives on the site.

To see the bridge materialize must have been gratifying. At 1,595 feet in length, supported by two massive granite towers, four steel cables, and an enormous web of suspending wires, the Brooklyn Bridge is perhaps the most graceful span ever built. On its opening day in 1883, more than one million spectators gathered to watch a

Caroline Louisa Frankenberg (left) and Margarethe Meyer Schurz each started a German model kindergarten in the United States in the 1850s. Both thus had a hand in starting what became an indispensable part of the American school system.

group of luminaries (including President Chester A. Arthur) take the first walk across the East River. In 1983, a similarly festive pageant marked the bridge's centennial with fireworks and the start of a campaign to erect a statue of the three Roeblings—John, Washington, and Emily—who brought the dream to fruition.

The Education of Americans

Which woman—Caroline Louisa Frankenberg or Margarethe Meyer Schurz (wife of political activist Carl Schurz)—was the first kindergarten teacher in the United States? Sources favoring Frankenberg say that in 1838 she arrived in Columbus, Ohio, where three of her brothers and some family friends from Germany had settled, and in the same year opened the first kindergarten in the nation. Her first attempts failed, but 20 years later, after a return visit to Germany (where kindergartens originated and were catching on), she returned to Ohio and succeeded. Her fee for each pupil was still only 75 cents per week, so she had to supplement her income by selling embroidery and handmade lace.

When Frankenberg made her second attempt, in 1858, Margarethe Schurz's kindergarten in Watertown, Wisconsin, had been in existence for three years. She gathered together the children of nearby relatives in her house so her daughter Agatha might have the benefits of a kindergarten experience, like her peers in Germany.

It does not matter, really, which woman gets the honor. The idea gradually spread across the United States. Private schools that had been established by earlier German immigrants were the first to pick it up—bilingual schools in Newark, New Jersey; Detroit, Michigan; and Louisville, Kentucky, for example. Then, in 1873, the first kindergarten associated with a public school system was established, in St. Louis, Missouri. In just 10 years (from 1870 to 1880), the number of kindergartens in the United States rose from 12 to 400, dispersed over 30 states. Today it is hard to imagine an elementary school without a kindergarten classroom.

Designers and artists trained at the Bauhaus (literally, house of building) were prominent among the generation of German immigrants in the 1920s and early 1930s. Walter Gropius, founder of the Bauhaus, asked his students to consider the social implications of architecture.

More recently, teachers formed the second-largest group of professionals fleeing Hitler's Germany, and American schools across the country worked to make room for them. Some institutions, such as the Institute for Advanced Study, in Princeton, and the New School for Social Research, in New York City, created special programs to aid refugee scholars. Alvin Johnson, founder of the New School, noted that on the lists of dismissed professors were "the names of nearly all the social scientists who had any creative spirit in them." From this observation he conceived the idea of a "University in Exile" that would form the school's graduate program in political and social sciences. By 1940, there were 60 émigré scholars on the New School's faculty. Black Mountain College, an experimental liberal arts school in North Carolina, became a rural refuge for many émigré writers, designers, and artists.

The Brain Gain

When Hitler rose to power, a vast number of people, mostly Jews, left Germany. By the end of 1937, an estimated 150,000 Germans had fled; Christians who openly opposed Nazism were also forced to flee. Initially, these refugees headed for neighboring countries, but as German armies overwhelmed much of Europe, they sought refuge overseas—in Palestine, China, South America. Between 1933 and 1945, 130,000 Germans came to the United States.

In many ways, of course, members of this group resembled earlier immigrants. At first, they struggled with problems of language and unfamiliar customs. Like their predecessors, they formed organizations of their own, sought American citizenship, and settled all over the country. But in some ways the refugees differed as a group from earlier immigrants.

World War II refugees did not come to the United States for economic reasons; they came to escape persecution. They tended to belong to the middle or upper classes, and, unlike their forebears, many were highly educated. In fact, so many prominent men and women came to the United States in the World War II era that historians have called it a "cultural" and "intellectual" migration, a "brain drain" from Europe. The achievements of World War II refugees do indeed crown a long list of German contributions to almost every discipline in America.

Artists and the Bauhaus

One émigré instructor at Black Mountain College was Josef Albers, an abstract painter. Albers, born in 1888 and trained in Germany, came with his wife, Anni, a textiles weaver and designer, to teach at Black Mountain in 1934. He later taught at Yale University in Connecticut. Most of Albers's work centered on color theory—the intensity of pigments and how they function with one another. His painting *Homage to the Square: Ascending* shows a yellow square within a white square within a gray square within a blue square. As the title suggests, the effect is one of ascent, of movement outward toward the

Ludwig Mies van der Rohe, the second director of the Bauhaus and one of the most influential architects in the world, fled Germany in 1933. The Seagram Building on Park Avenue in New York City, codesigned by Mies and Philip Johnson in 1958, is considered the pinnacle of the International Style.

Albert Einstein, born in Ulm, Germany, plays the violin on board ship to the United States in 1933. Though a pacifist, Einstein lent his abilities to an important American war project—harnessing atomic power. After the bombing of Hiroshima and Nagasaki, Japan, he advocated that atomic energy be used only for peaceful purposes.

edges of the canvas. The simple design also draws the viewer's attention to such basics as line, angle, shape, and space; like the many other works in Albers's *Homage to the Square* series, it invites contemplation of the realm shared by geometry and art and of the many subtle variations to be culled from a single theme.

The group of émigrés to which the Alberses belonged included people from all over Europe. Their art and design showed a fondness for breaking down traditional barriers, a propensity that drew them at one time or another to the Bauhaus (translated literally as "house of building"), a school of art established in Berlin by Walter Gropius in 1919 and moved to Dessau in 1925.

"The atmosphere at the Bauhaus," writes historian Peter Gay, "was curious, exhilarating: the Bauhaus was a family, a school, a cooperative business, a missionary society." Gropius gathered teachers and students together in what he called a laboratory, where "students stimulated teachers" and "every teacher was free as to how and what to teach." Classes and craft workshops were supplemented by contact with industry, in keeping with the school's slogan (Art and Technology—the New Unit) and with Gropius's view of the machine as the "modern medium of design." Through encountering the machine, not shying away from it, Gropius aimed "to restore architecture and design of today as a social art," to develop what he called "total architecture."

In the hope that his resignation would lessen the government's hostility toward the school, Gropius left the Bauhaus in 1928. The next director, Ludwig Mies van der Rohe, had received his first lessons in construction from his father, a stonemason. (Later Mies would say that "architecture begins when you place two bricks *carefully* together.") Like Gropius, he was eventually forced to leave Germany: in 1933 the Nazi regime's ascent led Mies to close the Bauhaus and flee to Switzerland. In 1938, he joined his former colleagues in the United States.

Though the unique atmosphere of the Bauhaus was never recreated in the United States, its two directors came to have a lasting influence on American architecture. Both developed teaching programs: Gropius at Harvard, Mies at Chicago's Armour Institute (now the Illinois Institute of Technology). Mies's course of studies moved rigorously from the most basic skills (students started with problems in ruling lines) to investigations of proportion and space, of how to plan a room, a building, a city. Mies himself left his mark on his adopted city, earning his reputation as "the poet of steel and glass" with apartment houses he designed for Chicago's lakefront and buildings on the campus at the Institute of Technology.

Gropius, who settled on the East Coast, asked his students to consider the social implications of architecture. What effect, for example, would a particular arrangement of windows, doors, and staircases have on a building's occupants? He also taught that problems of design were best met through collaboration; group effort was responsible for the design of the Harvard Graduate Center in Cambridge and the Children's Hospital Medical Center Complex, the National Shawmut Bank, and Temple Israel in Boston.

Gropius's students at the Bauhaus included Marcel Breuer. In 1924, at the age of 22, Breuer was inspired by the curved handlebars of his bicycle to create what remains his most familiar design: the tubular-steel chair. In 1938, after a successful career in Berlin and London, he joined his former teacher at Harvard. They remained partners until 1942, combining the Bauhaus style with the wood and stone of New England to build some of the most architecturally influential homes of the modern period. One of these is Breuer's own house in Lincoln, Massachusetts.

Einstein took U.S. citizenship in 1933 and soon began teaching in American universities. His special and general theories of relativity completely altered the way physicists think about time and space.

Einstein's Reach

The excitement surrounding Albert Einstein's trip to New York in 1921 was startling. With a fellow Jew, Chaim Weizmann, he was touring the United States to help raise money for Hebrew University, to be built in Jerusalem. Everywhere he went, he was greeted as a celebrity: Jews especially were anxious to catch a glimpse of the man who was being hailed as the Isaac Newton of the 20th century. He visited the White House, and overflow crowds everywhere came to hear him lecture—in German—on the theory of relativity.

Einstein (1879–1955) wrote about his own fame in a letter to a friend: "For my own part, I have always tended to solitude, a trait that usually becomes more pronounced with age. It is strange to be known so universally and yet to be so lonely." This was in September 1952, when Einstein was 73 years old.

At school, Einstein had detested the emphasis on rote memorization: "The teachers in the elementary school appeared to me like sergeants, and the Gymnasium teachers like lieutenants." Learning at home, however, had a great effect on him. As a grown man, he remembered two experiences in particular that drew him to the study of science. When he was 4 or 5, his father showed him a compass. "That this needle behaved in such a determined way did not at all fit into the nature of events. . . . Something deeply hidden had to be behind things," he wrote. And at 12, he encountered Euclidean geometry: "Here were assertions, as for example the intersections of the three altitudes of a triangle in one point, which—though by no means evident—could nevertheless be proved with such certainty that any doubt appeared to be out of the question." Thus, his childhood impressions revolved first around the mystery of the world, and second around the possibility of reaching some definite understanding of that mystery through mathematics.

Einstein's family was not well off. His father's business failed, causing the boy to leave school for a while and pursue his study of mathematics independently. Later, as a 16-year-old student at a Swiss school, he abandoned his study of pure mathematics in order to pursue physics. Here he got mixed reviews, preferring to study on his own or experiment in the laboratory rather than attend lectures. When he graduated, his teachers did not offer him an assistantship (a prerequisite for further training in physics), so he took a job at the patent office in Bern. Later Einstein would call the office "that secular cloister where I hatched my most beautiful ideas." Shortly thereafter he married Mileva Maric, a fellow student. They were so poor that, Einstein wrote, "In my theories I put a clock at every point of space, but in reality I can hardly afford one for my house."

But the imaginary clocks paid off. In 1905, Einstein published "On the Electrodynamics of Moving Bodies," his first scientific paper on special relativity. In this paper, he theorized that the speed of light is the greatest velocity in nature and that it is constant for all observers. This means that no matter how fast a person is moving, or in what direction, if he or she measures the speed of a light beam at any point of time, it will always be moving at 300,000 kilometers per second. On the other hand, any other motion is subject to change; everything else is *relative,* depending on the observer's frame of reference. Even time, mass, and space are not absolutes. This theory overthrew most previous approaches to physical science. With this and his later general theory of relativity, which took into account bodies moving at accelerated speed, Einstein introduced the idea that science does not produce definite conclusions but only "conjectures."

J. Robert Oppenheimer, born in New York City of German-Jewish parents, directed much of the wartime work in nuclear explosives and later headed the Institute for Advanced Study in Princeton, New Jersey.

Because of the innumerable shifting frames of reference in the universe, nothing can be proved decisively.

The immediate impact of this publication was a flurry of offers of teaching posts at European universities. In 1913, Einstein assumed the directorship of the newly planned Kaiser Wilhelm Institute for Theoretical Physics at the University of Berlin, and the stir over his theories quieted. But in 1919, a group of British astronomers traveled to South America to view an eclipse. In the course of their work, they verified one of Einstein's predictions: that starlight would bend, and that the sun—because it was such a large mass—would deflect starlight to a measurable degree. In November 1919, when the accuracy of his prediction was announced, Einstein became world famous.

Americans were particularly taken with Einstein. Throughout the 1920s, popularized versions of relativity abounded, but because of the difficulty of the theory, the average person was as much (if not more) drawn to the man as to his work and his reputation. Here was a pipe-smoking, violin-playing dreamer and Nobel Prize winner whose modesty fast became legendary: anyone lucky enough to reveal "something of the beauty of this mysterious universe," Einstein told one reporter, "should not . . . be personally celebrated."

In 1932, with anti-Semitism escalating in Germany (some of Einstein's papers on relativity were burned in a public square in Berlin), Einstein accepted an invitation to move to the United States and teach at the Institute for Advanced Study in Princeton. There he lived a relatively quiet life until his death in 1955.

Einstein spent his summers in Nassau Point, Long Island, where he sailed and played chamber music with neighbors. During the summer of 1939, he wrote to his friend Queen Elizabeth of Belgium that the war abroad greatly troubled him: "Except for the newspapers and the countless letters, I would hardly be aware that I live in a time when human inadequacy and cruelty are achieving frightful proportions." Although he was a pacifist (as a teenager he had renounced his German citizenship because he loathed the militarism of pre–World War I Germany), Einstein believed strongly that the only response to Hitler was armed confrontation. Aware of the military implications of the discovery of nuclear fission by his contemporaries, Einstein addressed a letter to President Franklin D. Roosevelt that same summer, urging him to support the work of American scientists in this field. After the defeat of Hitler and the destruction of Hiroshima by an atomic bomb with a design based on those discoveries, he urged that the bomb never be used again.

The Rocket Men

Two German-American scientists of the postwar era are particularly notable, both for their scientific work and for the partnership they helped create between government and science in the nuclear age: J. Robert Oppenheimer and Wernher von Braun. Oppenheimer, an American-born physicist of German-Jewish background, headed the Manhattan Project, the U.S. program to develop an explosive based on nuclear fission. After the war, he directed the Institute for Advanced Study in Princeton, New Jersey, until his death in 1967. His work with the government became an issue during the McCarthy trials of the early 1950s, in which he was unjustly labeled a suspected communist sympathizer.

Von Braun, a physicist, was responsible for the German V-2, the world's first operational guided missile; his work in the United States, however, focused not on missile design but on the development of rockets to launch the United States space program.

From one perspective, Wernher von Braun was a spoil of the war. He surrendered to Allied forces and emigrated voluntarily, arriving in Boston in September 1945 under the auspices of a program code-named "Project Paperclip," which aimed to persuade German scientists to emigrate to the United States. Despite controversy

Wernher von Braun's lifelong interest in developing a rocket that could fly to the moon was fulfilled when he and a team of German missile scientists came to the United States in 1945. They put the first U.S. satellite into orbit in 1958 and later devised the launch vehicle for the Apollo space program.

over this recruitment of former Nazi collaborators, the United States imported 652 "alien specialists" who settled in jobs in the military, industry, and academia between May 1945, a month after the war ended, and December 1952.

Even as a small boy, von Braun had been fascinated by the possibility of space travel. Encouraged first by his mother (who, for example, gave him a telescope as a confirmation gift) and then by the boarding school he attended (where he built an observatory), von Braun overcame his early difficulties with math and physics and began to study rocket engineering. As a high school student, he read Hermann Oberth's *The Rocket to Interplanetary Space,* which described the workings of a two-stage liquid-fueled rocket capable of breaking through Earth's gravitational field. In 1930, he entered the Berlin Institute of Technology and spent his spare time assisting Oberth in experiments. Aware that no private institution could support the costly research he envisioned, in 1932 von Braun became a civilian employee of the German army. Throughout the decade, he helped direct a team of scientists in the development of increasingly sophisticated rockets. The V-2 ("V" stands for *Vergeltungswaffe,* or "weapon of retribution"), the war's most powerful rocket, was successfully test launched from the Rocket Center at Peenemünde, on the Baltic Sea. This center was a joint enterprise of the German army and air force and was broken up after the British raid of 1943. In 1944, von Braun was imprisoned for two weeks by the Gestapo, the Nazi secret police, for voicing doubts about Germany's ability to win the war and for publicly expressing his desire to design a space rocket rather than a weapon.

In 1945 von Braun surrendered to American troops. As Charles L. Stewart, a special agent of Army Intelligence, told it, Magnus von Braun, Wernher's brother, emerged first from behind enemy lines. He reported that his brother and some 150 other top German rocket personnel "wished to join the Americans to continue their work in rocket development." They had selected the United States, he said, because "this country was the one most able to provide the resources required for interplanetary travel." All the captured Peenemünde personnel were detained at a ski resort, where the atmosphere was more like that of a symposium than a prisoner-of-war camp. Wind-tunnel specialists and rocket engineers willingly shared their ideas and equipment designs with American officials.

In 1958, after a decade spent on weapons research, von Braun's desire to put his talents to use for space exploration rather than destruction was fulfilled. On January 31, 1958, he and his rocket team placed the first American satellite, *Encounter 1,* into orbit. The group was soon transferred to the National Aeronautics and Space Administration (NASA), where it became the core of the George C. Marshall Space Flight Center, in Huntsville, Alabama. Here, von Braun and his staff developed the Saturn 5 rocket launch vehicle, which in July 1969, lifted *Apollo 11* on its path to the moon. Von Braun was named assistant director of NASA in 1970. After the 9 flights and 6 lunar landings of the Apollo spacecraft program were completed in 1972, he retired.

TICKET OFFICE

A German-American marching band, Cincinnati, Ohio, about 1890. Music is still usually in the spotlight at gatherings of German Americans.

A FINAL NOTE

In an 1852 edition of his *Journal of Music*, critic John Sullivan Dwight applauded the performance of the Germania Musical Society, then touring the United States:

> The growing taste for pure instrumental music, at so many points in our wide country, has been greatly indebted for the last three or four years to the flying visits of this model abridgement of an orchestra. Though hardly twenty-four in number, these young artists have diffused among our people something nearer than we have before had, a true idea of German music, both in its popular and in its classic forms.

One of the most resonant and lasting aspects of German culture in America has been its music. From choral societies to brass bands to symphony orchestras, music has been an essential part of the German immigrant's life. Even today, a German-American celebration without music is a rarity. Advertisements in German-language newspapers urging readers to gather for traditional German food, drink, and dancing often highlight the band as the evening's main attraction. In Philadelphia and other cities, a *Mannerchor*, or men's chorus, still sings at well-attended performances. And audiences in concert halls everywhere applaud musicians of German heritage playing music by German composers.

For German Americans, music has served to bridge the old country and the new, and to unite members of the ethnic group who come from widely diverse regions of German-speaking lands. In the 20th century, as Germans dispersed throughout the United States and Canada, the cultural element that traveled most easily was music: the baroque works of Johann Sebastian Bach, the giant of choral and sacred music; the classicism of Wolfgang Amadeus Mozart and Joseph Haydn; and the great German Romantic tradition of Ludwig von Beethoven, Franz Schubert, Robert Schumann, Johannes Brahms, and Richard Wagner. During the years of heavy German immigration, thousands of German Americans could play, sing, or merely listen to these works, at home or in local halls and clubs. Others wrote and adapted folk songs, marches, and church music for their neighbors and fellow countrymen. Music was the German Americans' province—they so dominated orchestral music in America in the 19th century that, in 1890, 89 of the 94 performers in the New York Philharmonic were German-born.

Sadly, popular interest in symphonies and operas is no longer so broad-based. Today Germans are still amply represented on the concert stage, but the majority of Americans prefer popular or electronic music to the standard classical favorites of past generations. Even German-American marching bands are as likely to play pieces by John Philip Sousa or theme songs from movies as they are to play pieces by one of their great forebears. Amateur singing clubs reflect this shift, too. The Liederkranz Society of New York City, founded in 1847, sings the works of German and non-German composers, in both German and English. There are decades-old Liederkranz clubs in Philadelphia and Chicago, and new clubs have sprung up in suburban Long Island, New York, and in Florida, where very few of the choristers are native German-speakers. Just as the German tongue has given way to English, so has Ger-

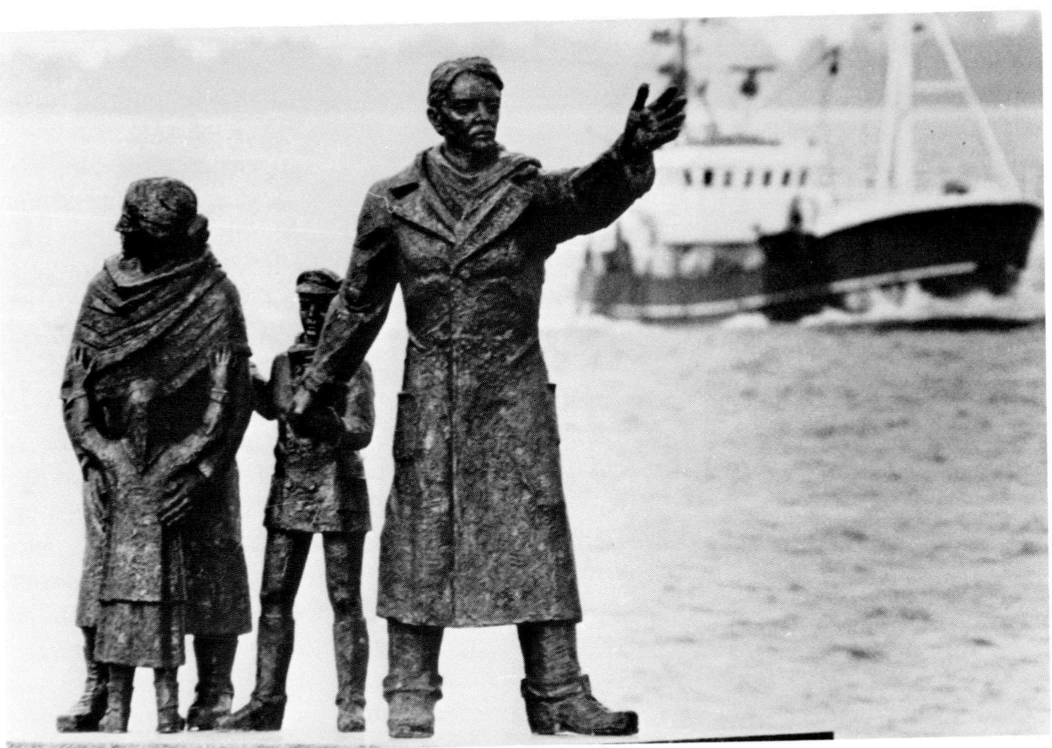

This bronze statue, Parents with Two Children, *paid for by German Americans, stands by the harbor of the German port city of Bremerhaven. Emigration from Germany to America has been continuous for the last 300 years.*

man music yielded to typically American tunes. Yet whatever the music's origins, its airing at parades and spring festivals still transmits a sense of German tradition.

Despite the persistence of this one tradition, however, ethnic consciousness among German Americans has been on the wane for decades. Immigration from Germany fell off dramatically after the influx of World War II refugees, and by 1972, most American residents who called themselves German were at least third-generation Americans. Other factors, including the diversity of the immigrants and their rapid assimilation into American society, have worked against efforts to keep the sense of German-American community at a high level. Strong Amish and Mennonite communities, especially in Pennsylvania, retain much of their 350-year-old culture; but the members' group identity is rooted more in their religion than in their Germanness.

The lack of ethnic consciousness among German Americans has had positive effects; for example, in recent decades there have been virtually no conflicts between German Americans and other American ethnic groups. But the near disappearance of a discrete German-American culture indicates that complete assimilation demands a profound trade-off, one that includes not only the abandonment of Old World hatreds and chauvinisms but the loss of traditional languages and art forms. Ethnic consciousness among German Americans may be taking a new form, however, rooted not so much in the German language but in the festivity of coming together to proclaim their German heritage. The turnout at Steuben Day parades, held every spring in many communities, and the popularity of German festivals are evidence that Americans of both German and non-German descent are interested in preserving German heritage.

Appeals for ethnic unity go out from organizations such as the German-American National Congress, or Deutsch-Amerikanisch National Kongress (DANK). Founded in 1959 and based in Chicago, DANK has 60 chapters across the United States that are "interested in promoting all that is best in German culture and in retaining the German language among Americans of German descent." These have been familiar aims throughout the history of emigration to America, but realizing them today is more difficult than ever—even though more than 44 million Americans claim some German ancestry. Indeed, one recent brochure directed at prospective members reads more like an urgent plea than an invitation to share in a common culture: "We must all work together so that our most priceless possession—our heritage and knowledge of our cultural contributions—will not be lost."

Further Reading

Cunz, Dieter. *They Came from Germany: The Stories of Famous German-Americans.* New York: Dodd, Mead, 1966.

Keith, Harold. *The Obstinate Land.* New York: Crowell, 1977.

Luebke, Frederick C. *Germans in the New World: Essays in the History of Immigration.* Urbana: University of Illinois Press, 1990.

Martin, George. *The Damrosch Dynasty.* Boston: Houghton Mifflin, 1983.

Miller, Randall, ed. *Germans in America: Retrospect and Prospect.* Philadelphia: The German Society of Philadelphia, 1984.

Muggamin, Howard. *The Jewish Americans.* New York: Chelsea House, 1996.

O'Connor, Richard. *The German-Americans.* New York: Little, Brown, 1968.

Parker, Steve. *Albert Einstein and Relativity.* New York: Chelsea House, 1995.

Rippley, La Vern. *The German-Americans.* Boston: Twayne, 1976.

Trefousse, Hans L. *Carl Schurz: A Biography.* Knoxville, University of Tennessee Press, 1982.

Wittke, Carl. *Refugees of Revolution: The German Forty-Eighters in America.* Philadelphia: University of Pennsylvania Press, 1952.

Wust, Klaus, and Heinz Moos, eds. *Three-Hundred Years of German Immigrants in North America, 1683–1983: A Pictorial History with 510 Illustrations.* Baltimore: Moos Publishing, 1983.

INDEX

ANNE GALICICH received a degree in English literature from Stanford University and currently teaches at Horace Mann School in New York City. She has been a science writer and editor and is the author of a biography of the late Samantha Smith, the grade school student from Maine whose visit to the Soviet Union in 1983 gained worldwide attention.

SANDRA STOTSKY is director of the Institute on Writing, Reading, and Civic Education at the Harvard Graduate School of Education as well as a research associate there. She is also editor of *Research in the Teaching of English,* a journal sponsored by the National Council of Teachers of English.

Dr. Stotsky holds a bachelor of arts degree with distinction from the University of Michigan and a doctorate in education from the Harvard Graduate School of Education. She has taught on the elementary and high school levels and at Northeastern University, Curry College, and Harvard. Her work in education has ranged from serving on academic advisory boards to developing elementary and secondary curricula as a consultant to the Polish Ministry of Education. She has written numerous scholarly articles, curricular materials, encyclopedia entries, and reviews and is the author or coauthor of three books on education.

MARY BARR SISSON has a bachelor of arts degree in English and American Language and Literature from Harvard-Radcliffe University. She currently lives in Queens, New York, and works as a writer and editor.

REED UEDA is associate professor of history at Tufts University. He graduated summa cum laude with a bachelor of arts degree from UCLA, received master of arts degrees from both the University of Chicago and Harvard University, and received a doctorate in history from Harvard.

Dr. Ueda was research editor of the *Harvard Encyclopedia of American Ethnic Groups* and has served on the board of editors for *American Quarterly, Harvard Educational Review, Journal of Interdisciplinary History,* and *University of Chicago School Review*. He is the author of several books on ethnic studies, including *Postwar Immigrant America: A Social History, Ethnic Groups in History Textbooks,* and *Immigration.*

DANIEL PATRICK MOYNIHAN is the senior United States senator from New York. He is also the only person in American history to serve in the cabinets or subcabinets of four successive presidents—Kennedy, Johnson, Nixon, and Ford. Formerly a professor of government at Harvard University, he has written and edited many books, including *Beyond the Melting Pot, Ethnicity: Theory and Experience* (both with Nathan Glazer), *Loyalties,* and *Family and Nation.*

PICTURE CREDITS

AP/Wide World Photos: p. 92; Balch Reproductions, The Balch Institute for Ethnic Studies: p. 86; The Bettmann Archive: pp. 21, 42, 103, 104, 110, 112, 114; Bildarchiv Preussischer Kulturbesitz: p. 70; Cincinnati Historical Society: pp. 61, 65, 118–119; Colonial Williamsburg: p. 51; Ezra Stoller Esto: p. 109; German Information Center: pp. 48, 49, 51, 53, 79, 97, 99, 101, 108, 121; H. J. Heinz Company: p. 76; Historical Society of Pennsylvania: p. 56; Institute of Texan Cultures: p. 12; The Kansas State Historical Society, Topeka: p. 63; Kunsthistorisches Museum, Vienna: p. 28; Library of Congress: pp. 18–19, 41, 44–45, 46, 89, 102; Maryland Historical Society: pp. 25, 39; Milwaukee County Historical Society: p. 88; Minnesota Historical Society: pp. 17, 64, 85; Museum of the City of New York: pp. 72–73; NASA: p. 116; National Archives: pp. 94–95; National Museum of American Art, Smithsonian Institution, Bequest of Helen Huntington Hull: pp. 54–55; National Park Service: p. 16; New York Historical Society: pp. 31, 83; New York Public Library Picture Collection: p. 32; New York Public Library, Rare Book Division, Astor, Lenox & Tilden Foundation: pp. 26, 34; New York State Historical Association, Cooperstown: p. 50; Ohio Historical Society: p. 106; Philadelphia Museum of Art: p. 35; Enoch Pratt Free Library: p. 98; Sophienburg Memorial Association: p. 59; State Historical Society, Bismarck, North Dakota: p. 74; State Historical Society of Wisconsin: pp. 58, 96, 106: UPI/Bettmann Newsphotos: pp. 67, 84, 93; Henry Francis du Pont Winterthur Museum: pp. 52, 53; Johann Wolff's *New Jagerbuch*: p. 20; Woodcarving by T. de Thulstrup after H. Jeannerat: p. 78; Woodcut by Eduard Kreyzschmar: p. 30.
Map (p. 15) by Gary Tong.
Cover photos courtesy of the Minnesota Historical Society and the National Park Service.